My name is
L.T.
AF583839

Are you ready to write?

Posture

Is your back resting against the chair?

Are your feet flat on the floor?

Paper position

left-handed

Are you holding the paper steady with your non-writing hand?

right-handed

Pencil grip

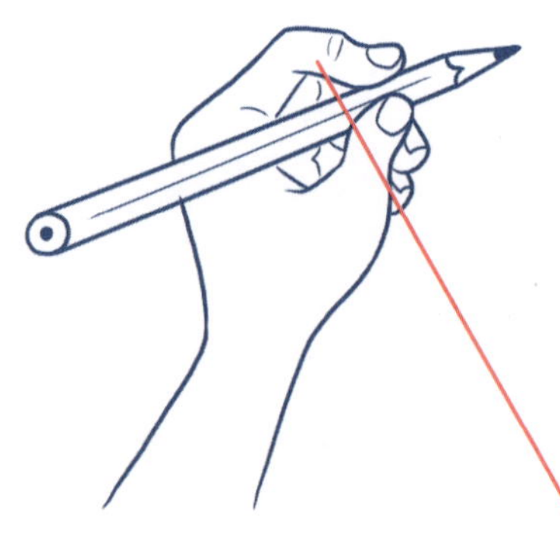

Is one finger on top of the pencil?

Left-handers, hold your pencil a little further up so you can see your handwriting!

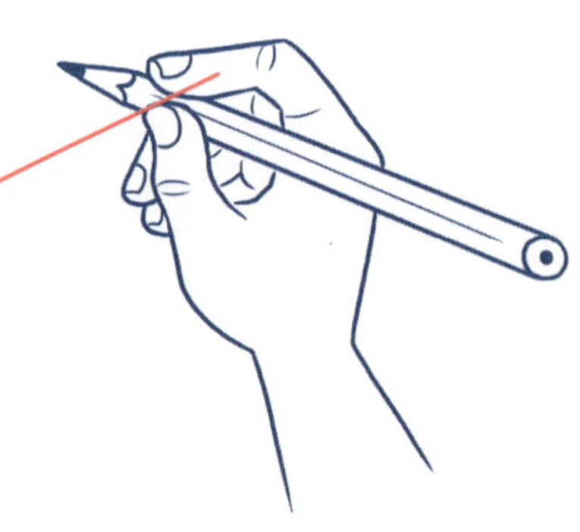

Start at the red dots. Follow the arrows.

Start at the red dots. Follow the arrows.

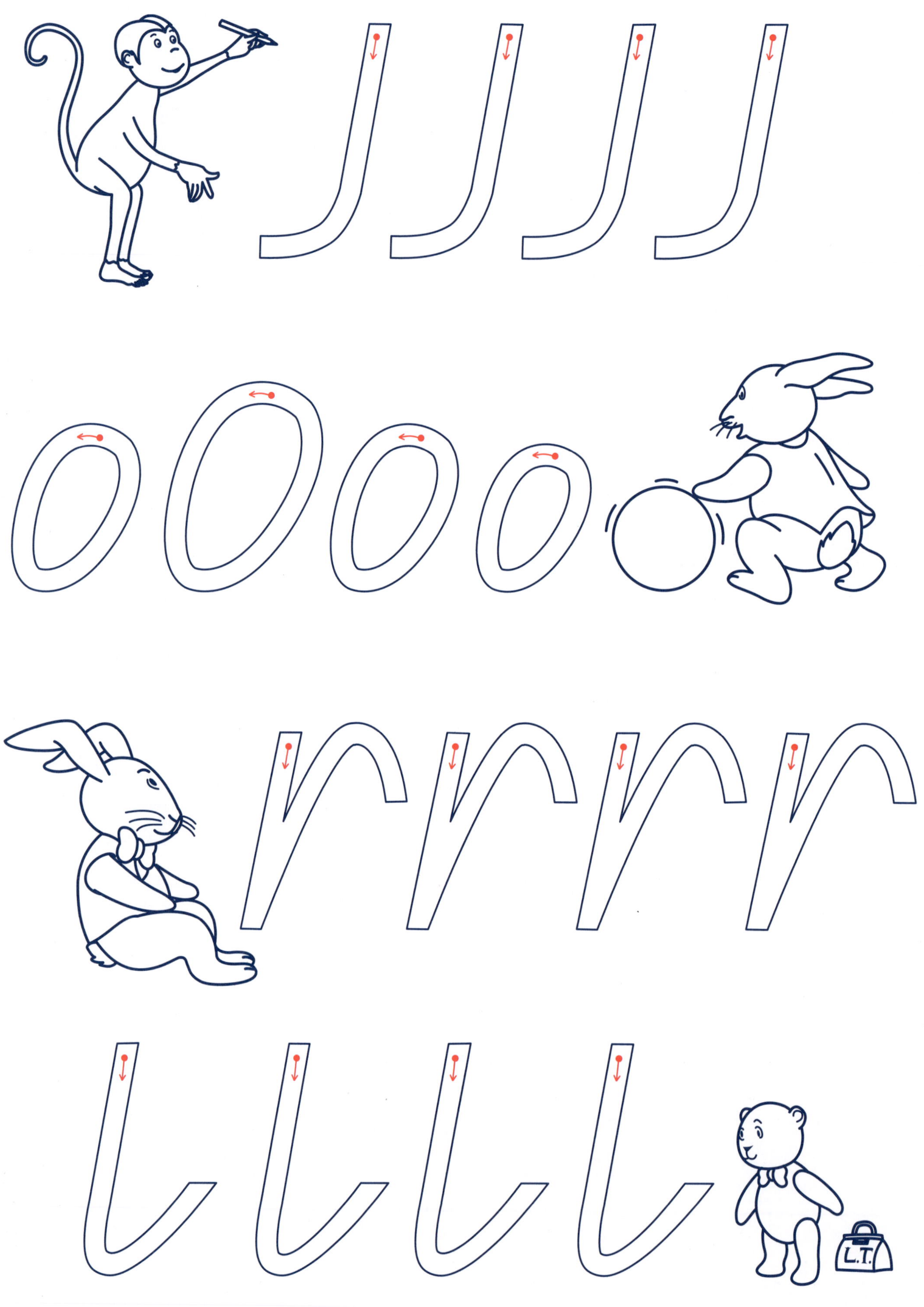

Start at the red dots. Follow the arrows.

Start at the red dots. Follow the arrows.

Start at the red dots. Follow the arrows.

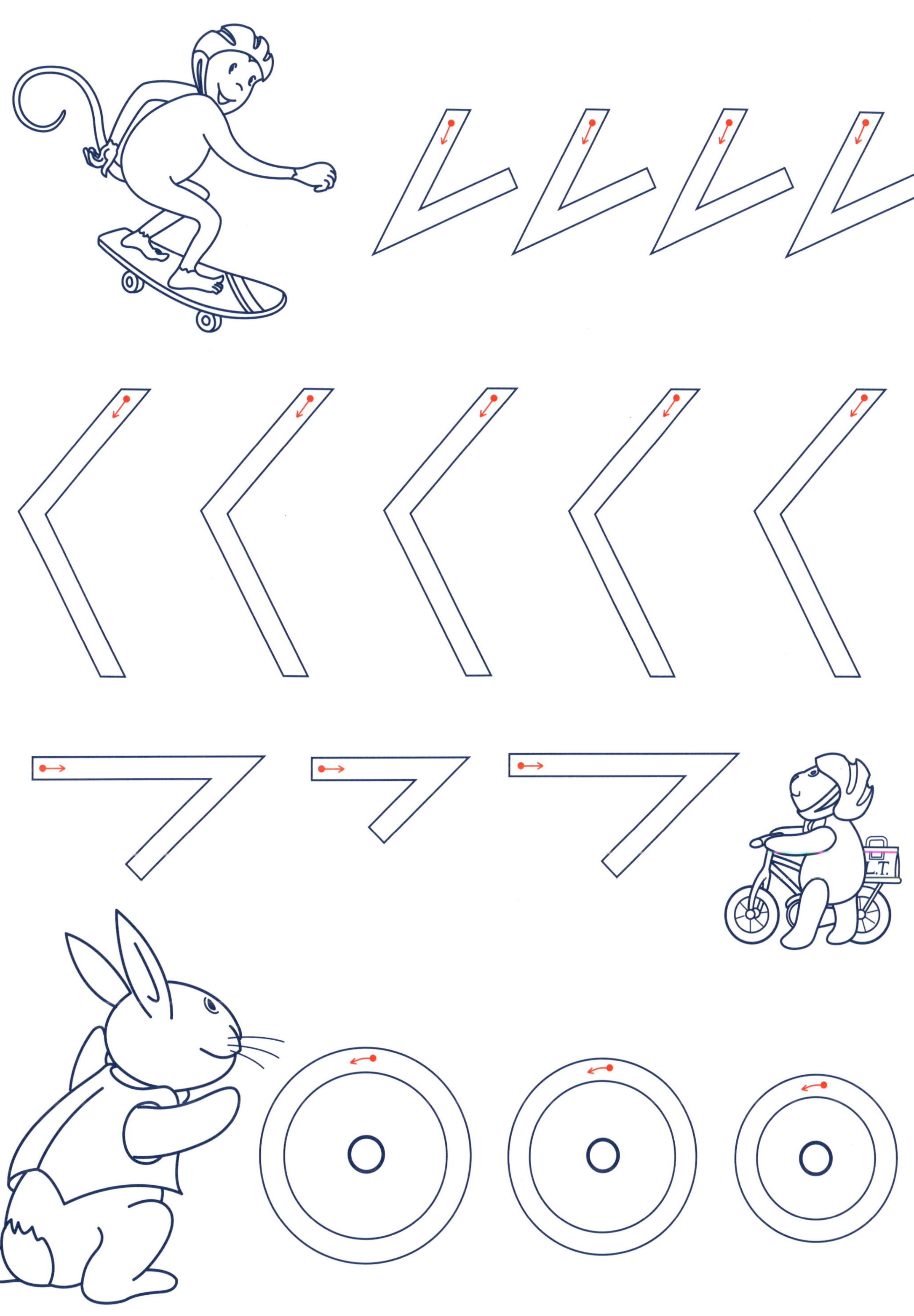

Start at the red dots. Follow the arrows.

Start at the red dots. Follow the arrows.

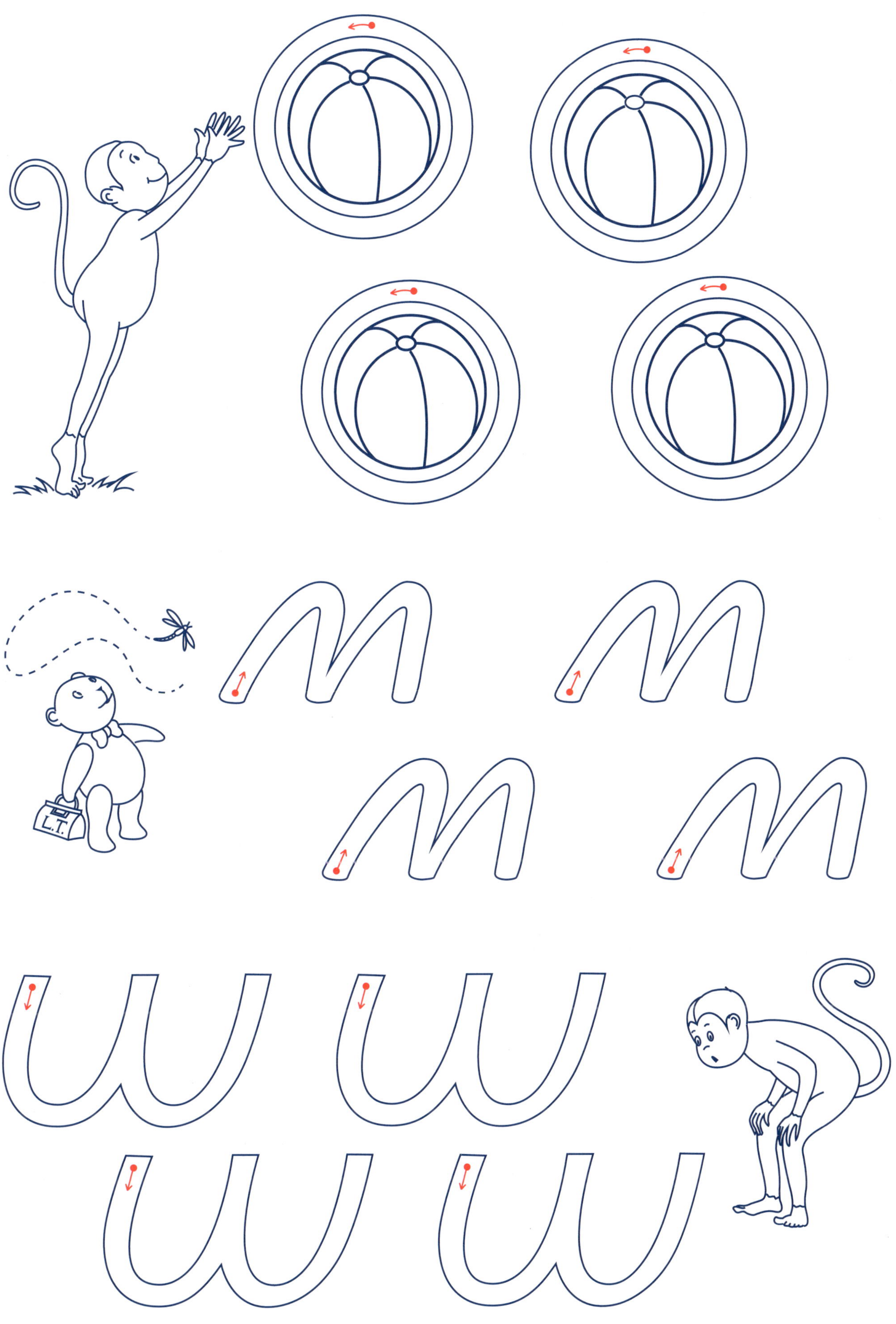

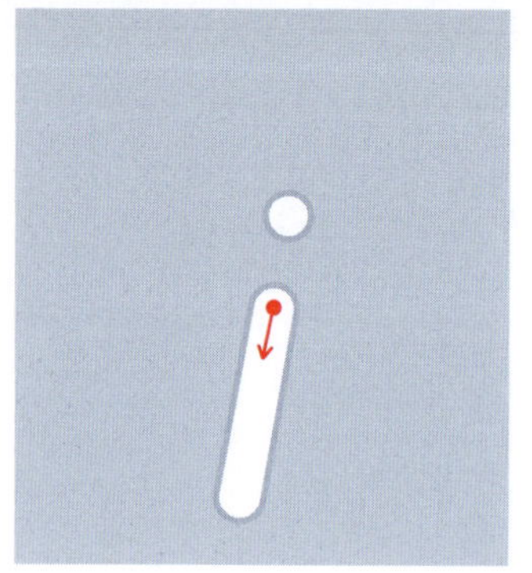

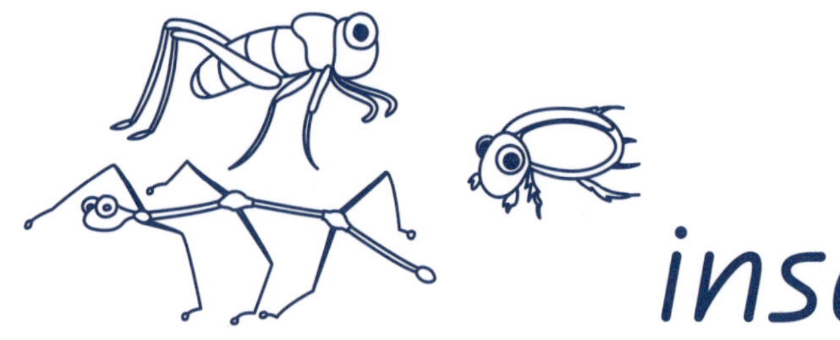

insects

Start at the red dot. Follow the arrow.

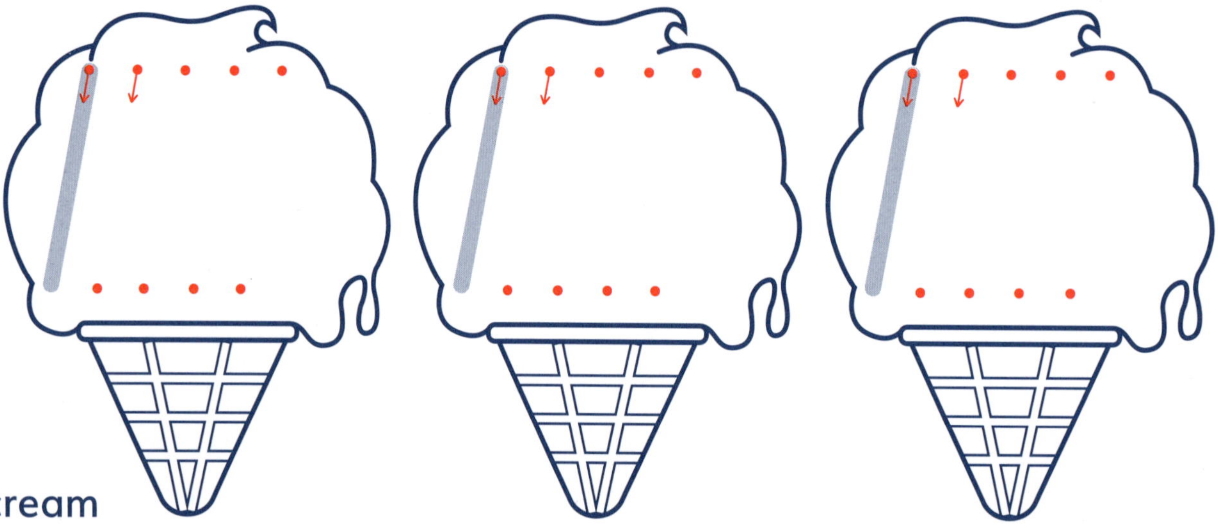

ice cream

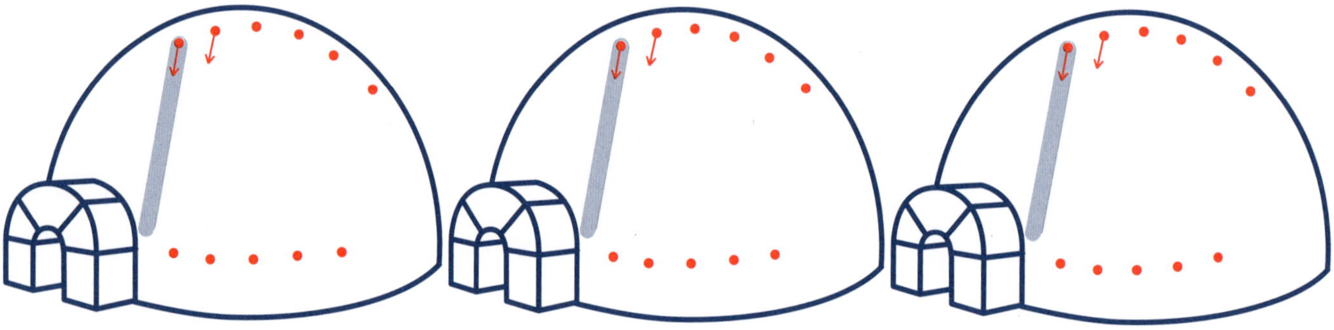

igloo

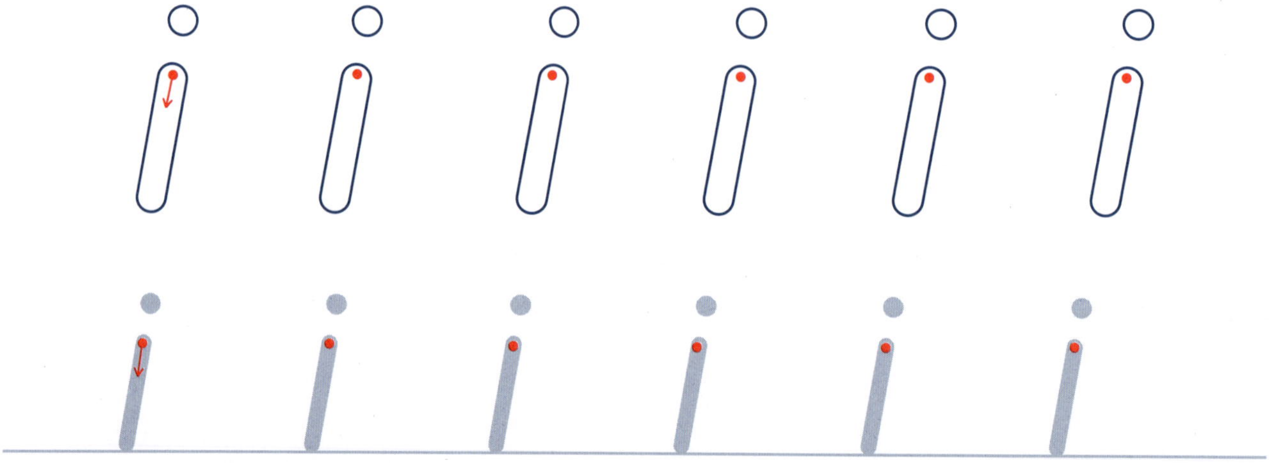

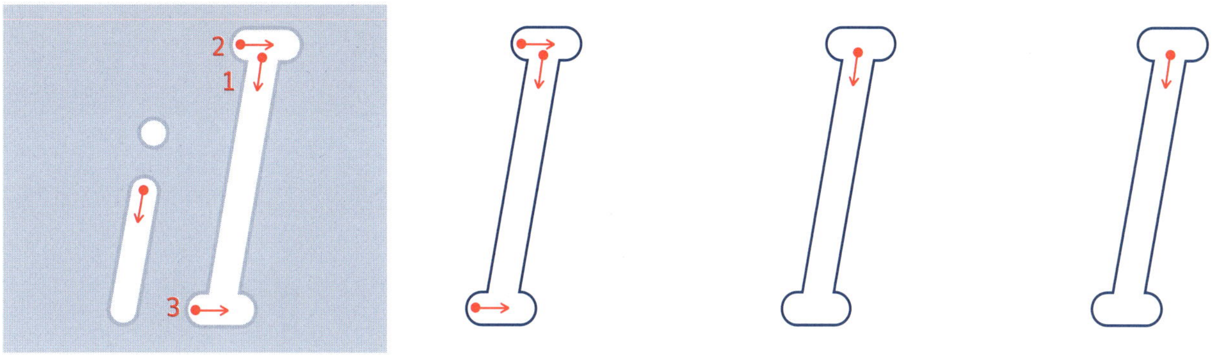

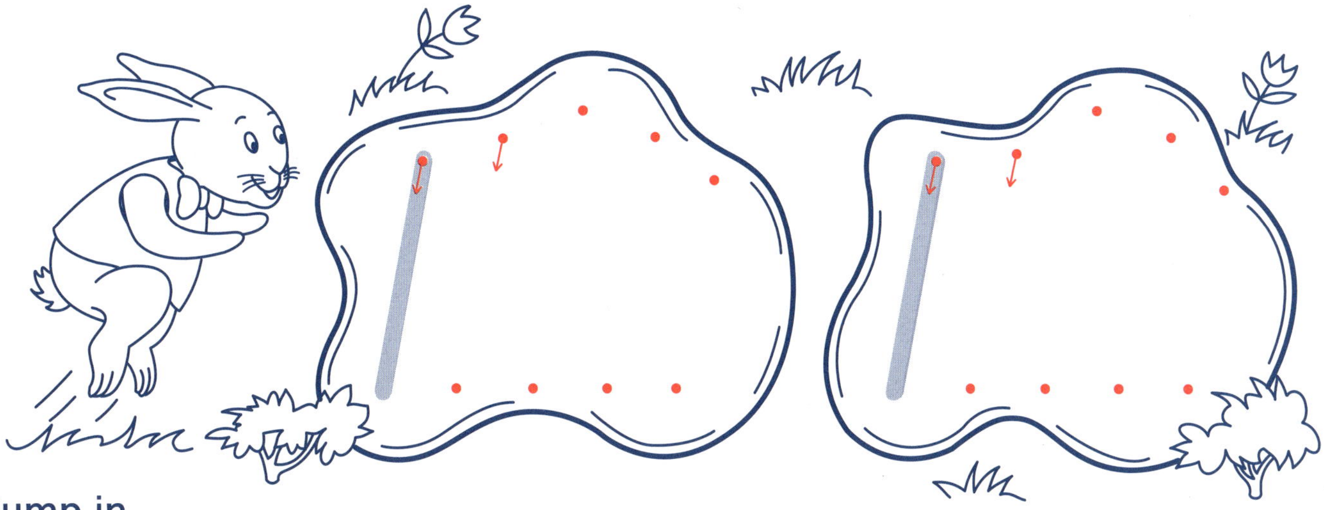

jump in

island

Trace the letter.

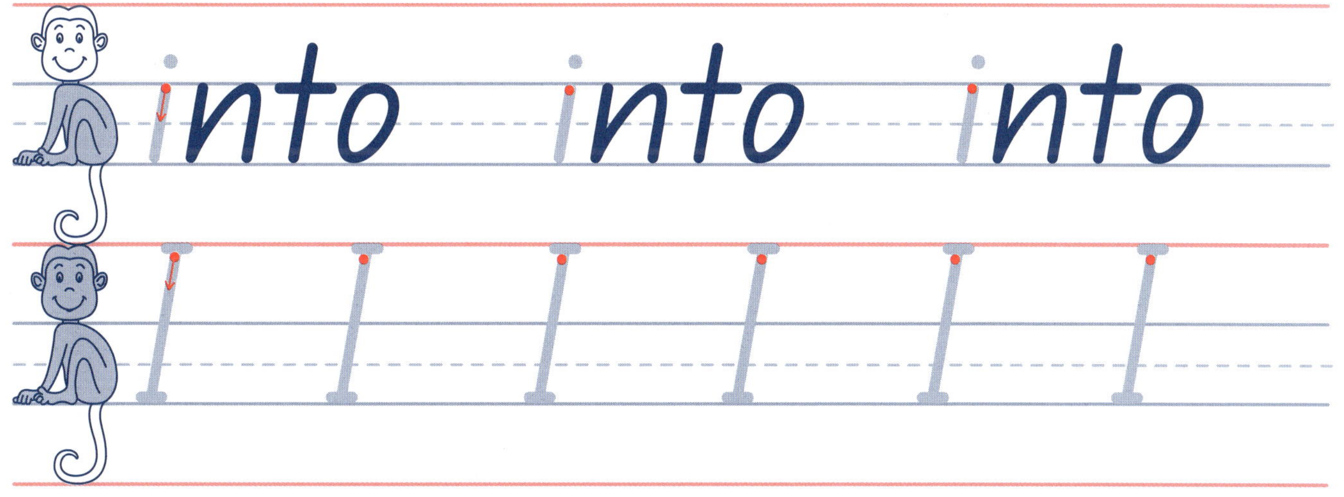

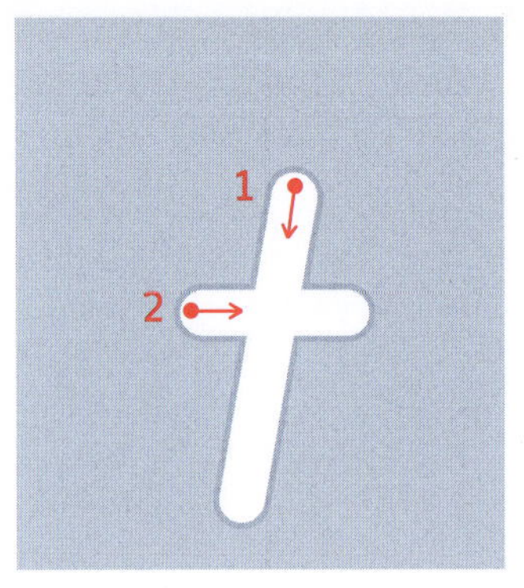

Start at the red dot. Follow the arrow.

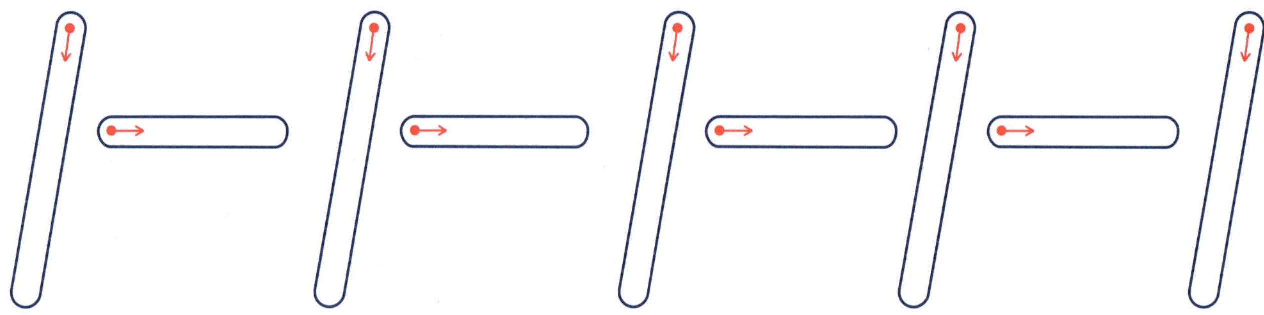

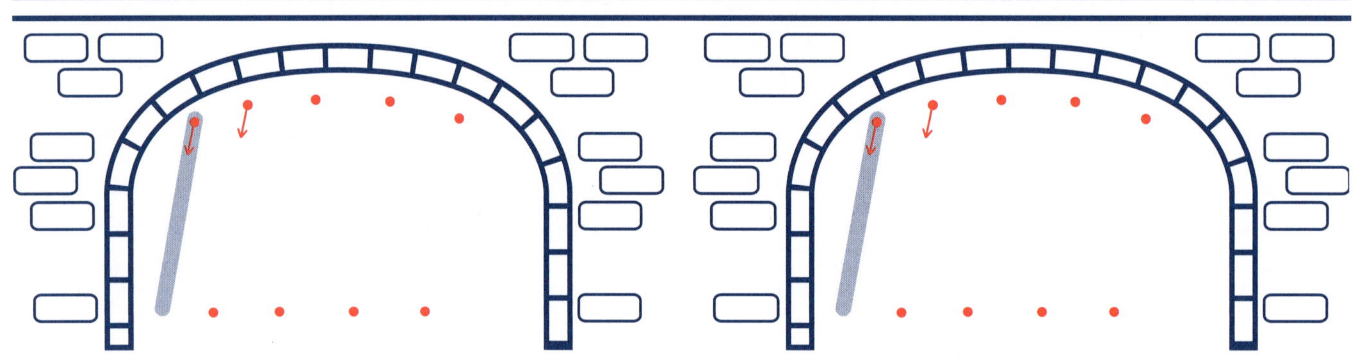

tunnels

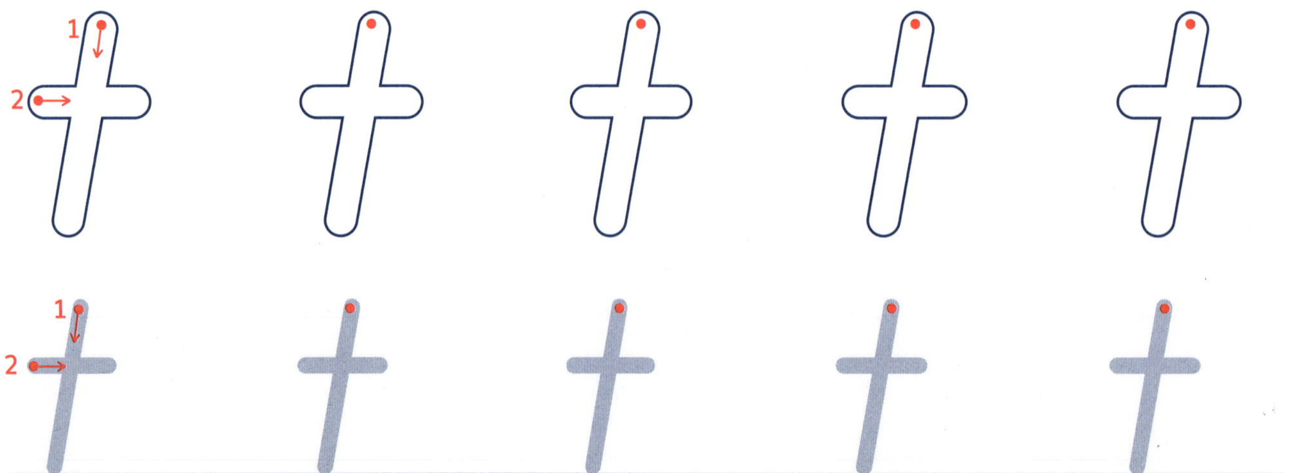

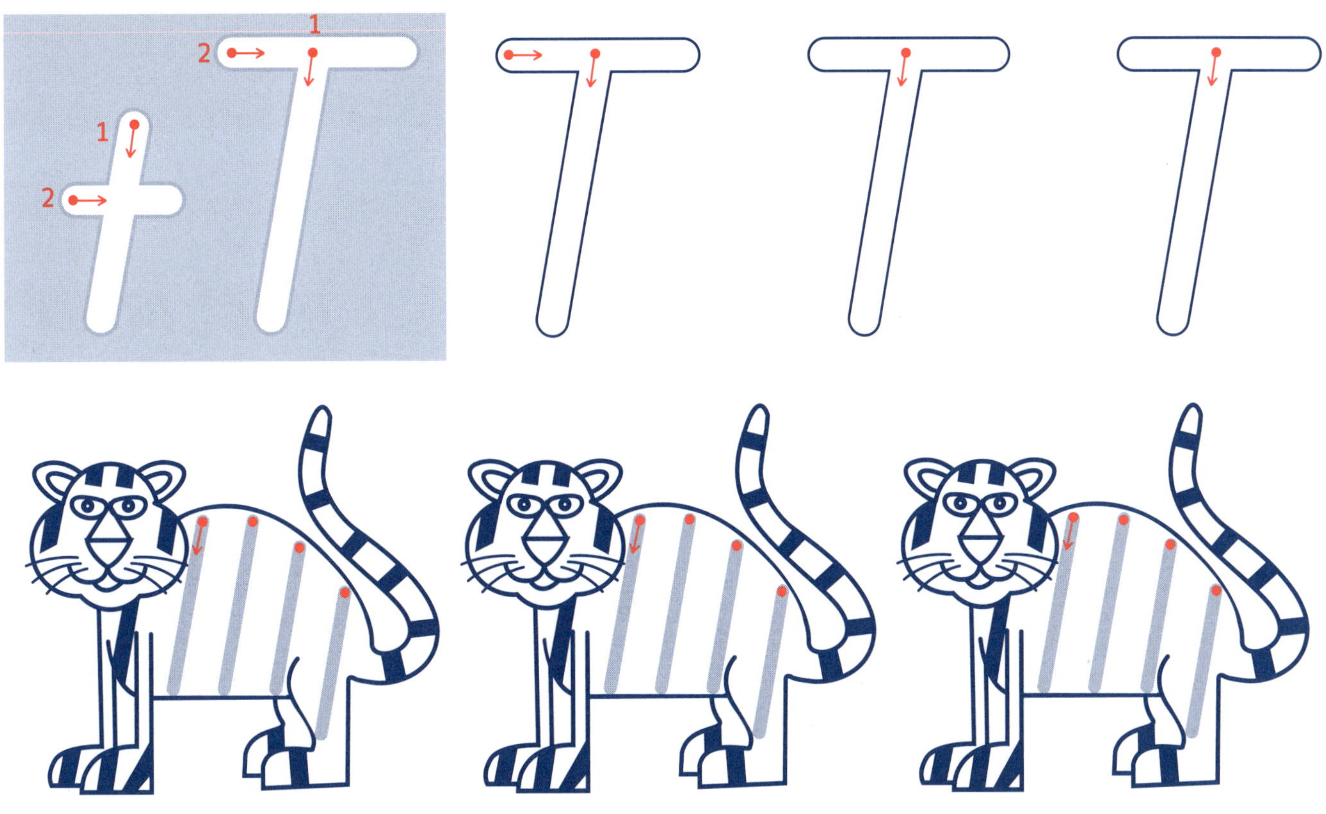

tiger

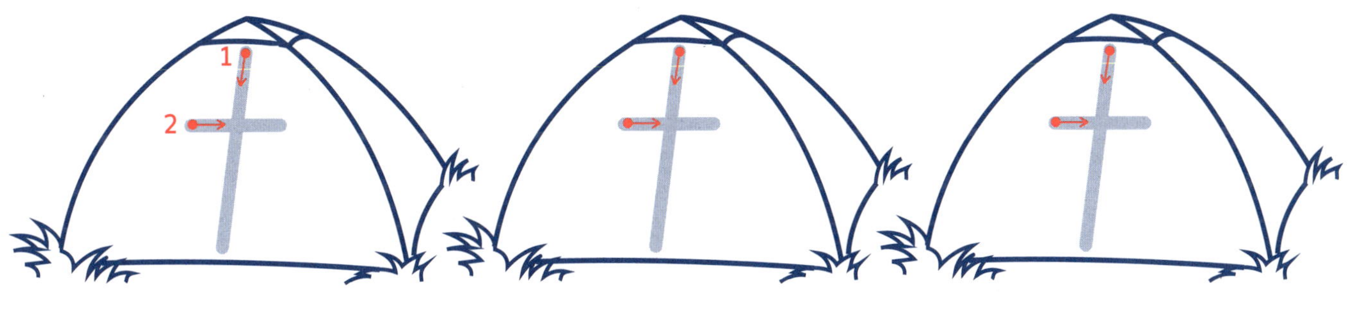

tent

Trace the letter.

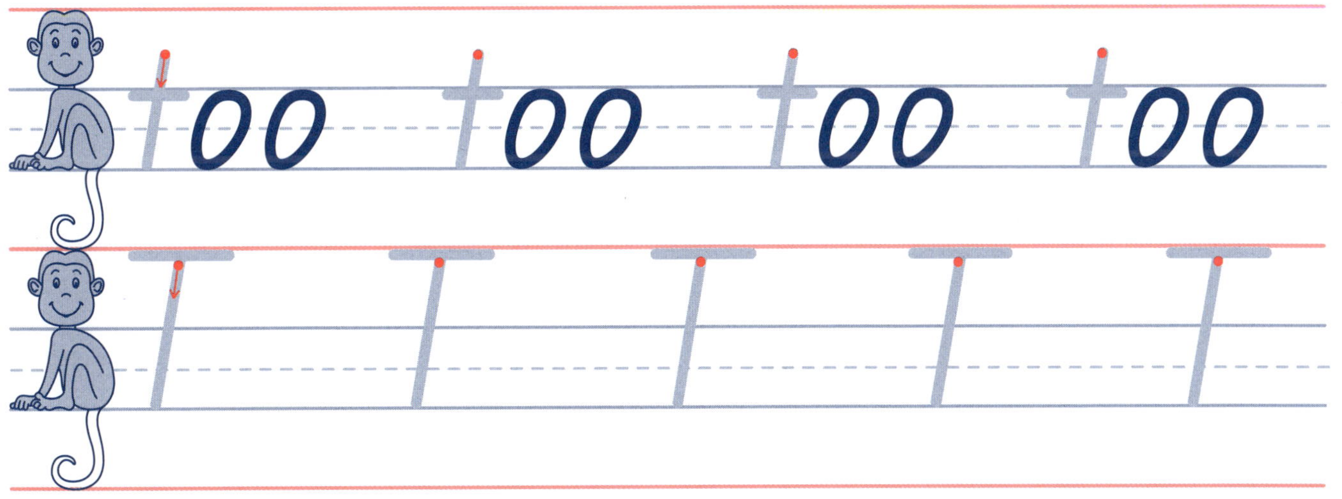

ladder

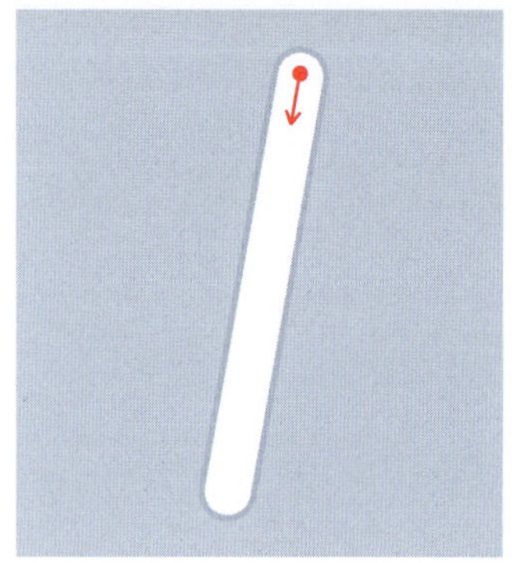

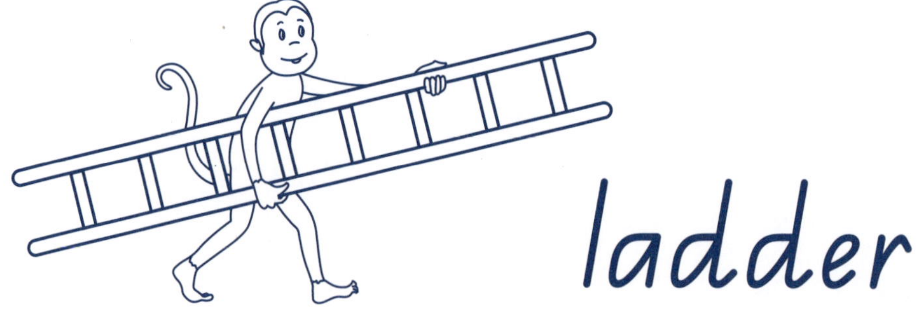

Start at the red dot. Follow the arrow.

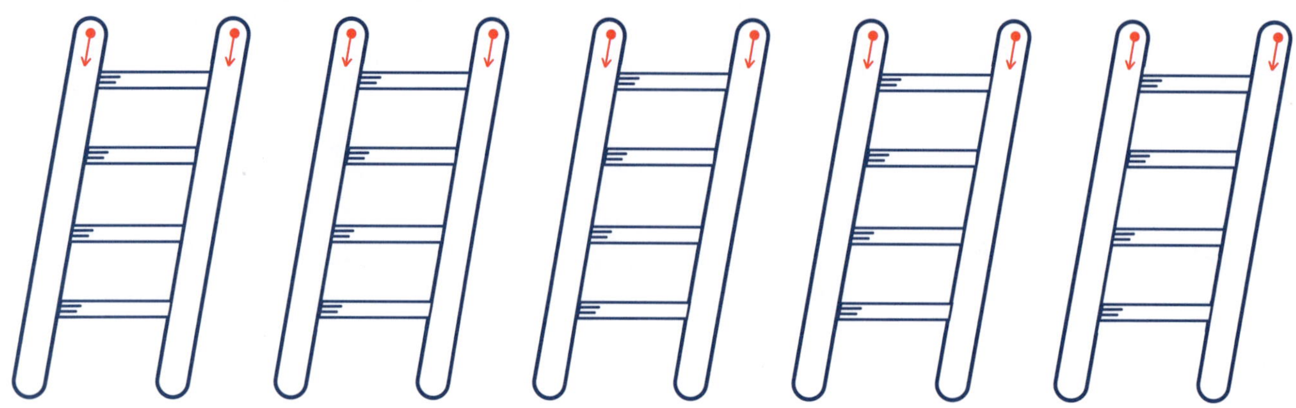

ladder

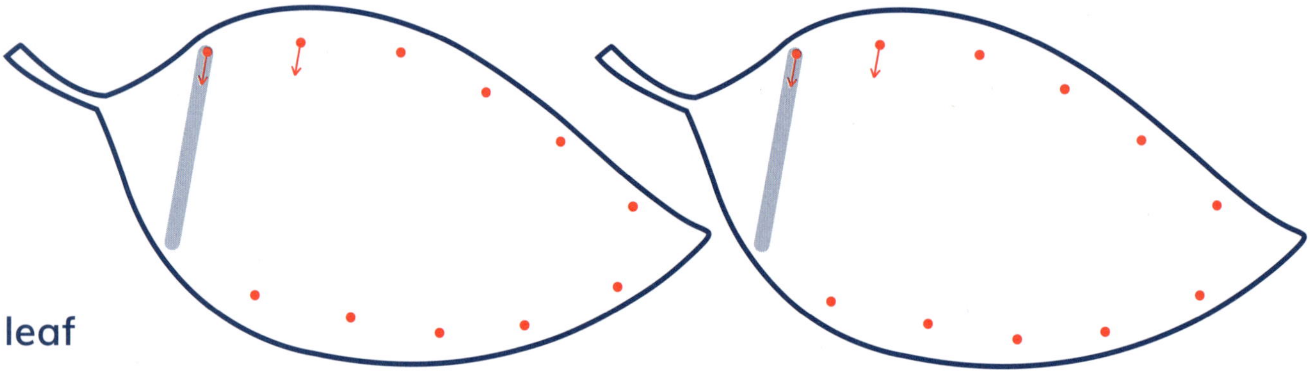

leaf

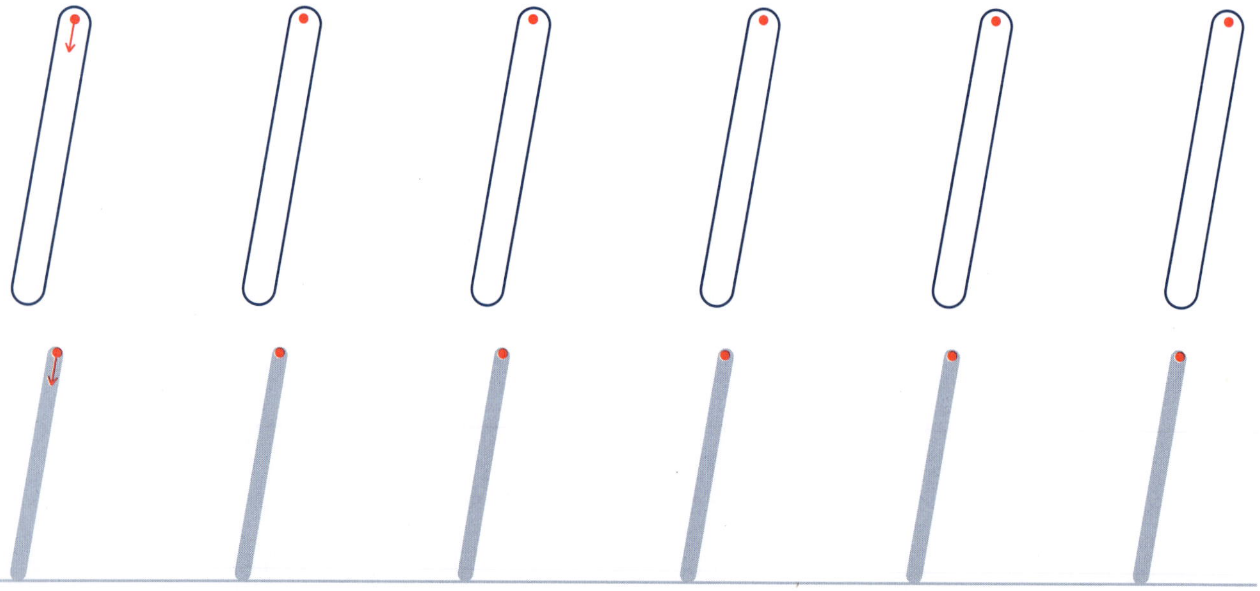

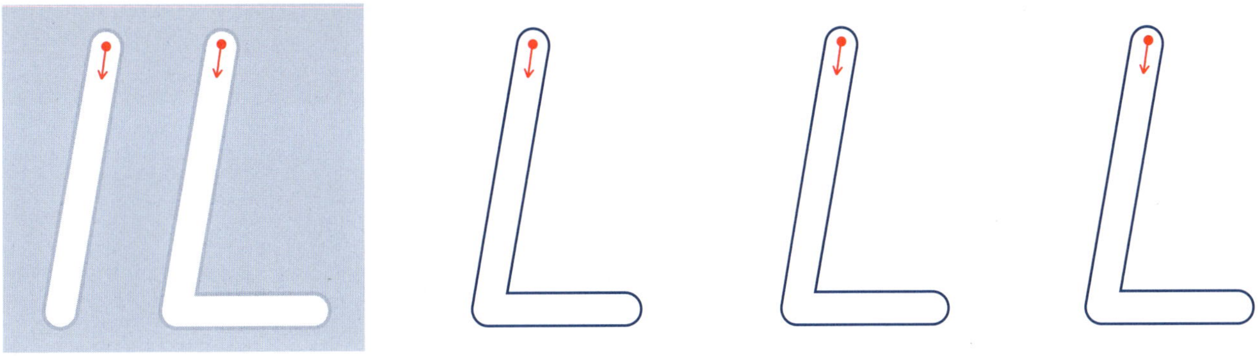

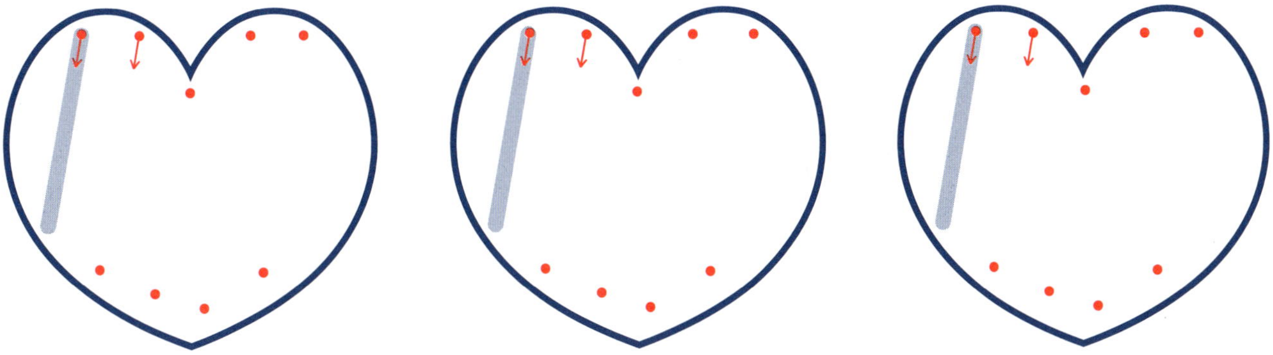

l L L L L

love

lollipop

Trace the letter.

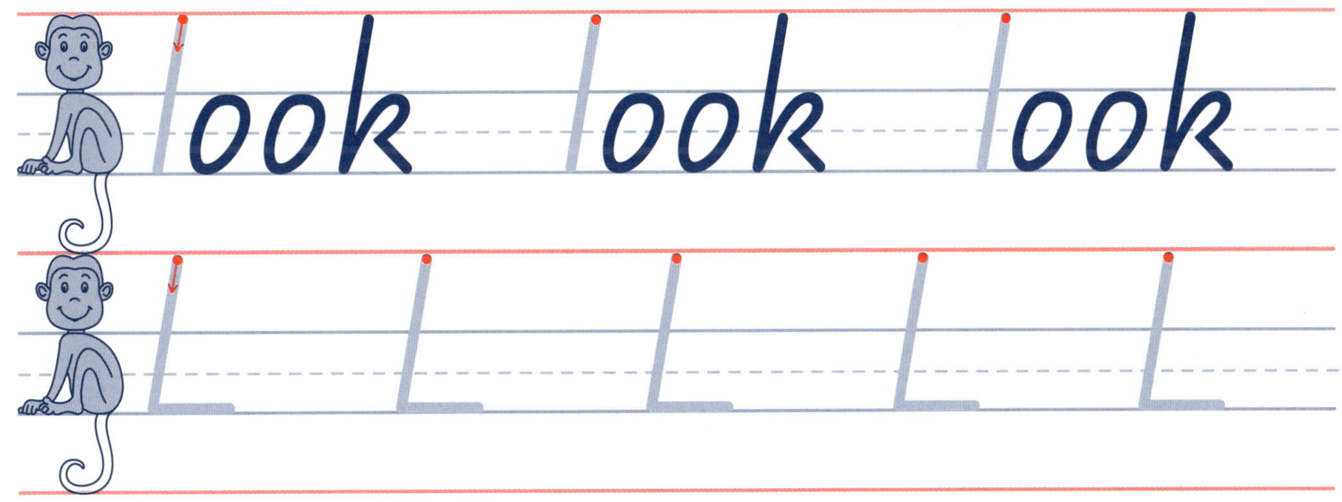

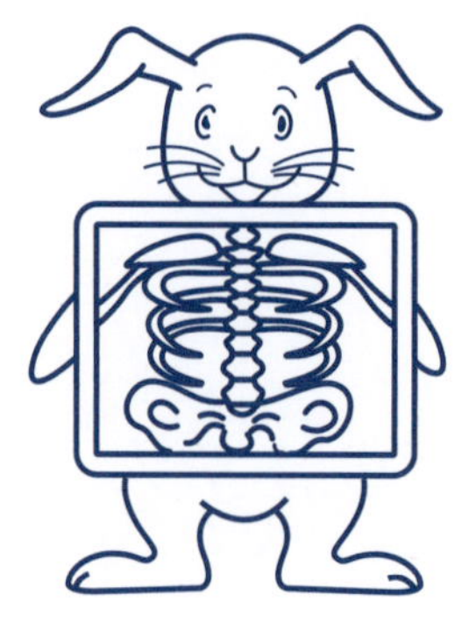

x-ray

Start at the red dot. Follow the arrow.

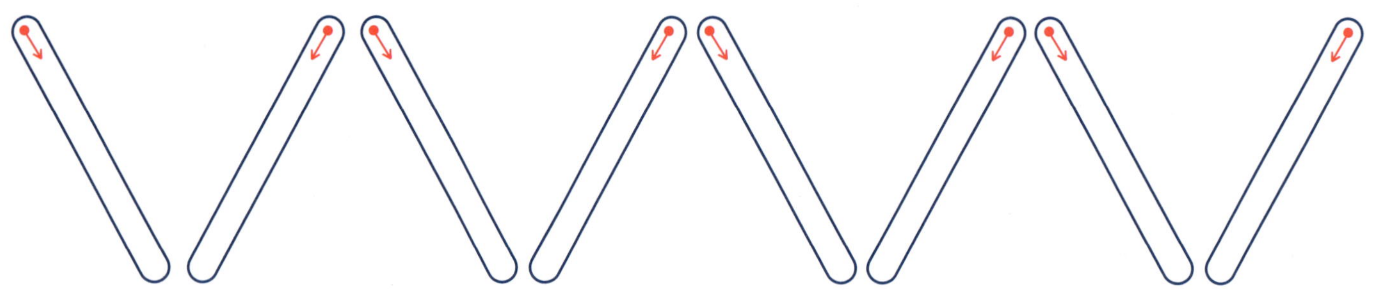

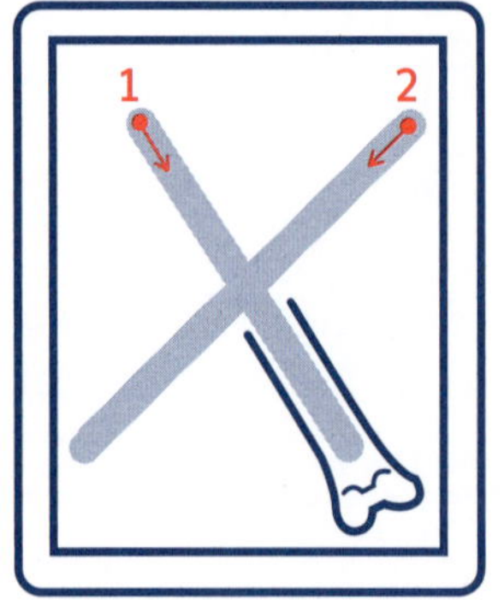

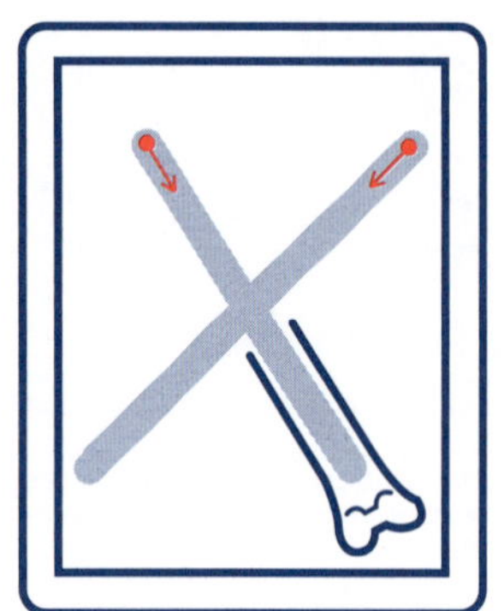

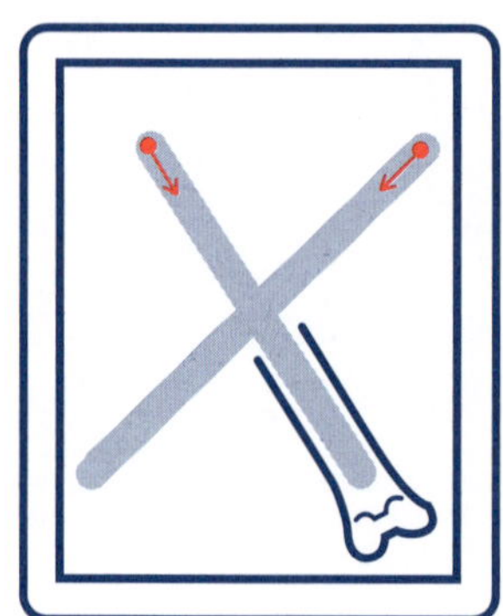

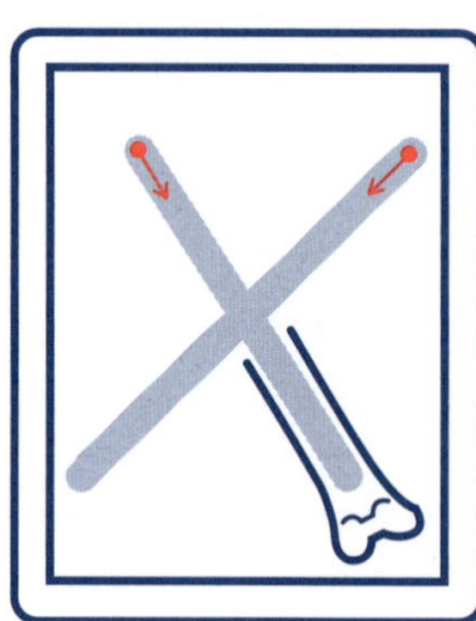

x-ray

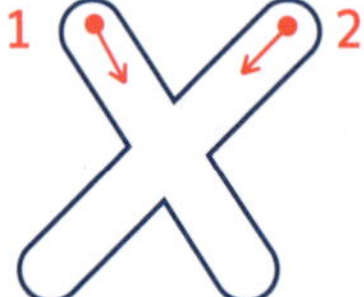

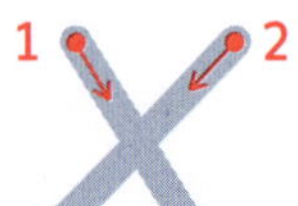

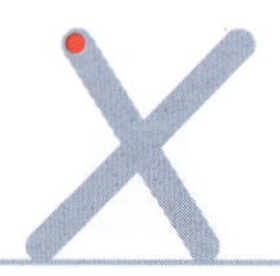

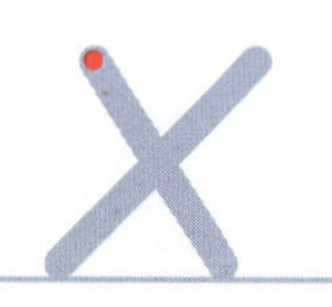

1 2 1 2

box

Trace the letter.

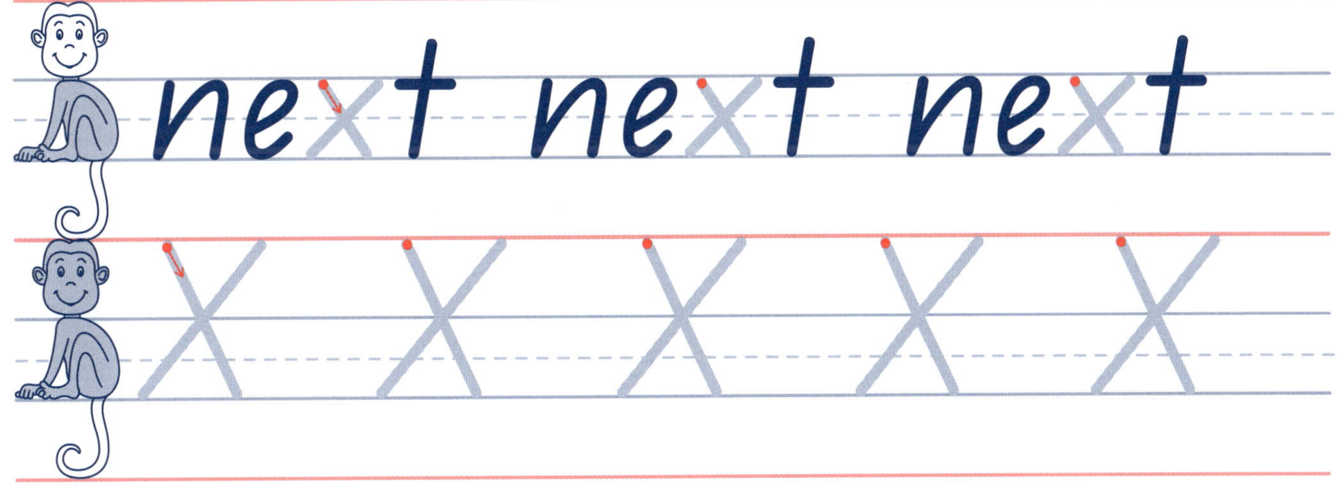

z

zoo

Start at the red dot. Follow the arrow.

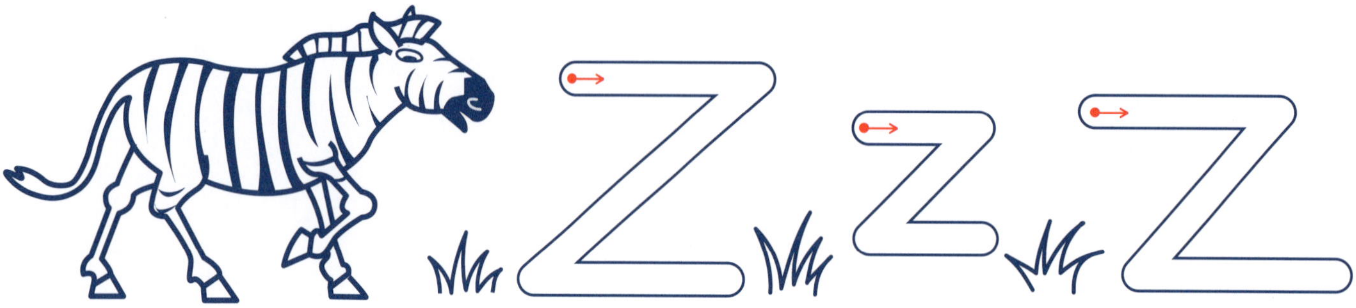

zebra

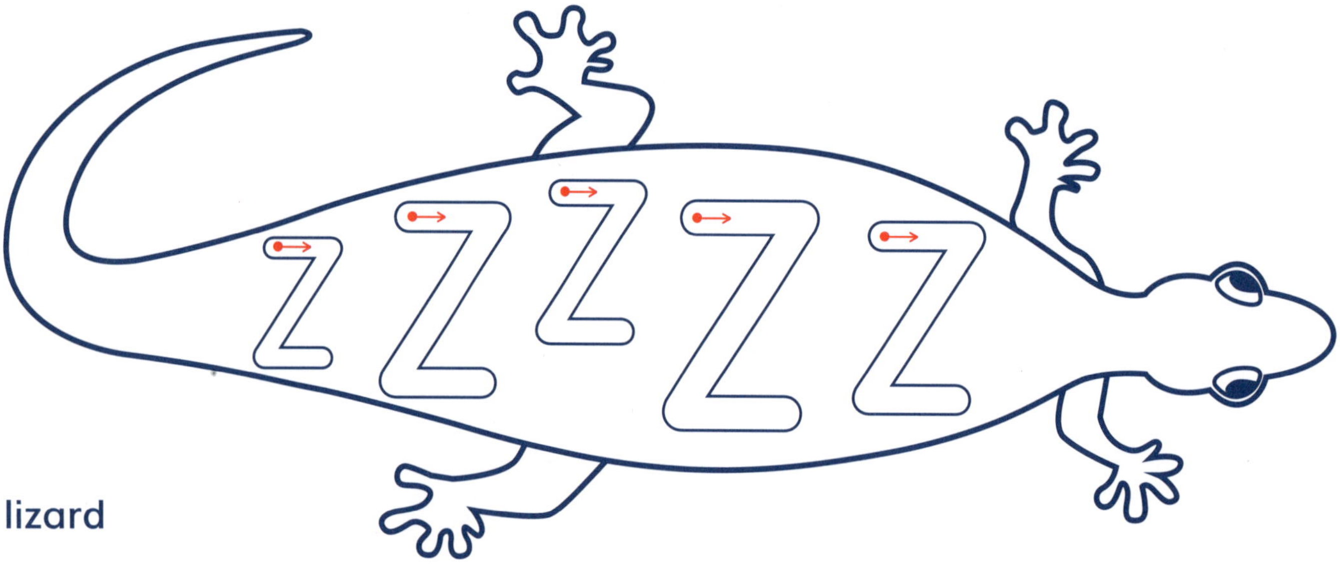

lizard

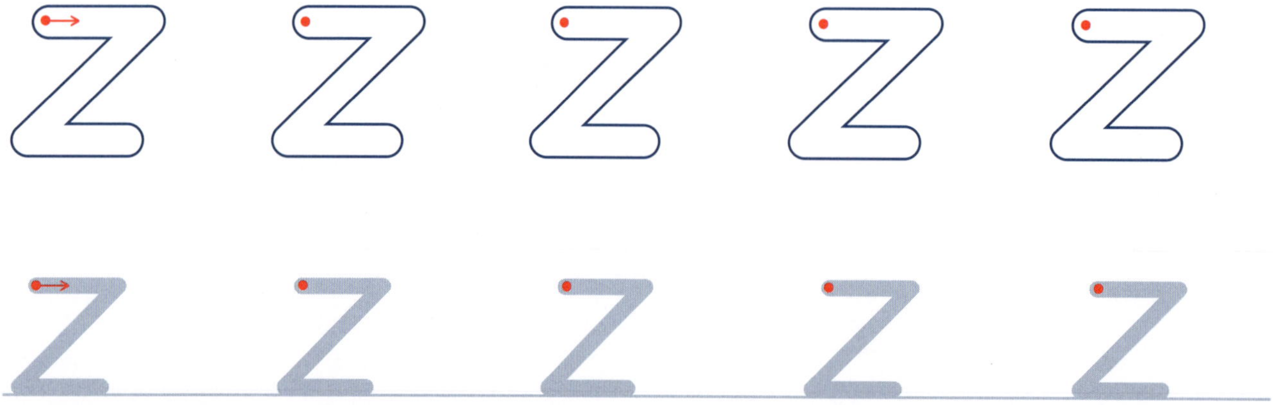

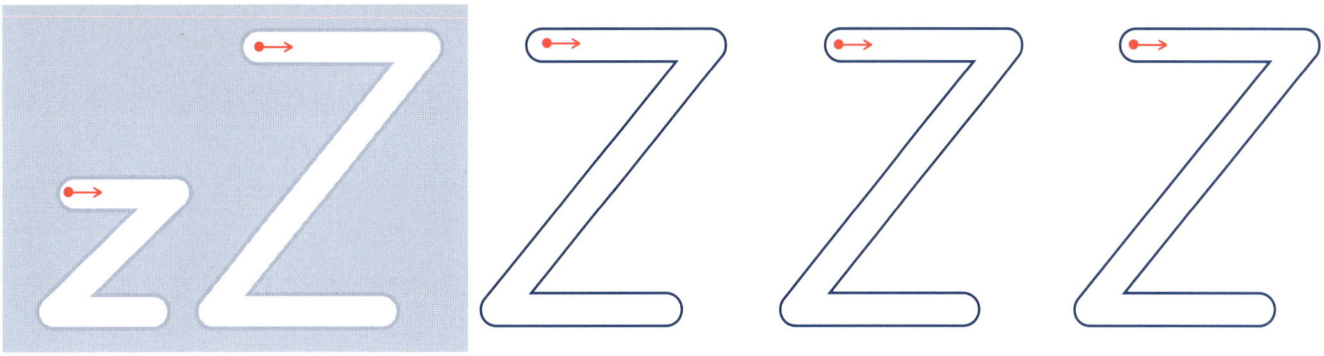

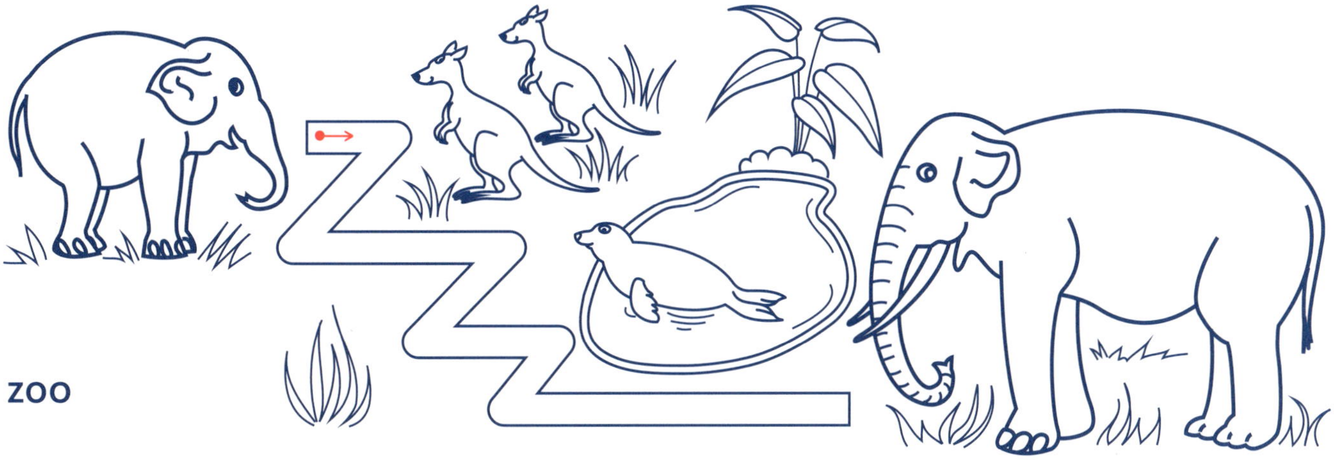

zZ Z Z Z

zoo

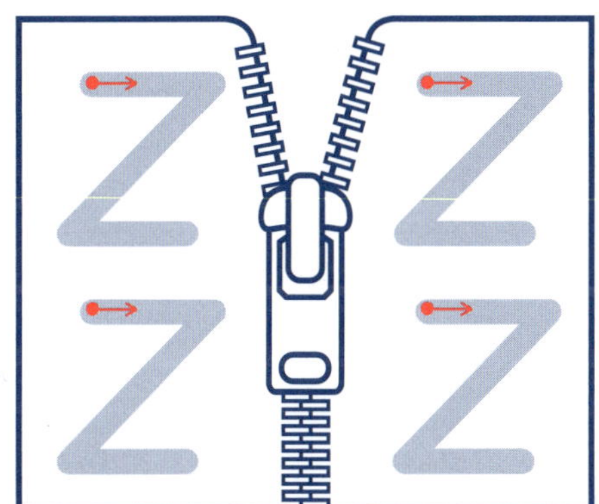
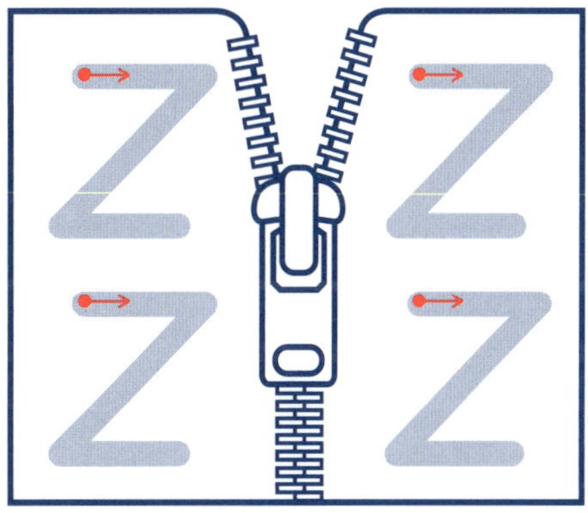

zip

Trace the letter.

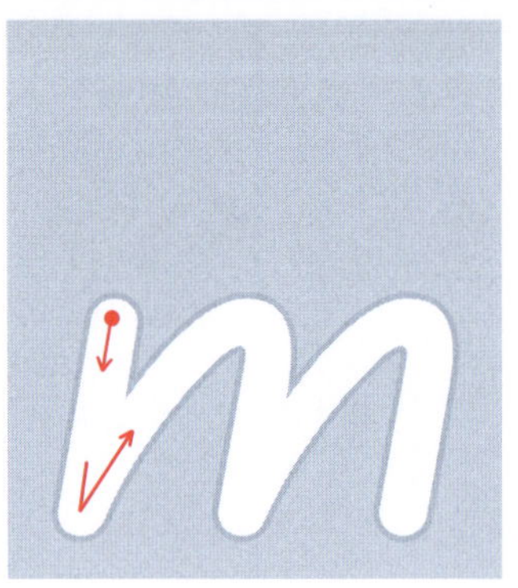

mouse

Start at the red dot. Follow the arrow.

moon

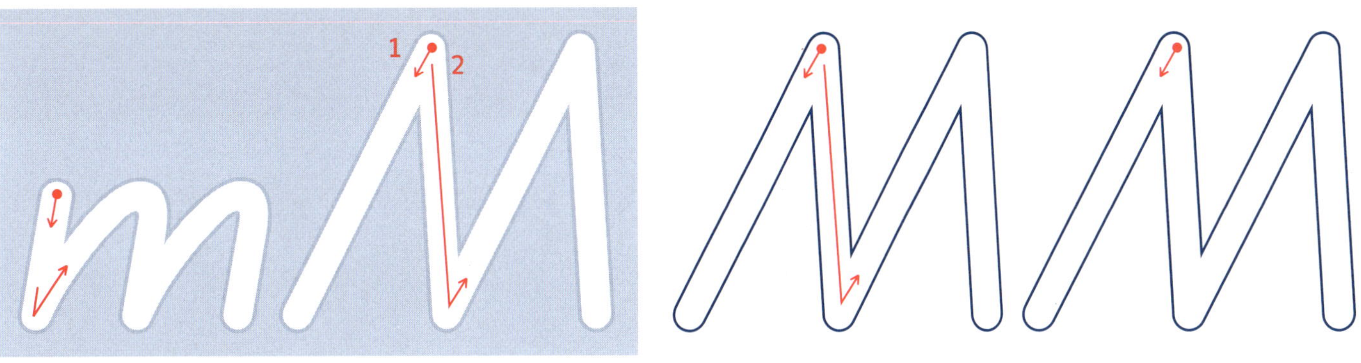

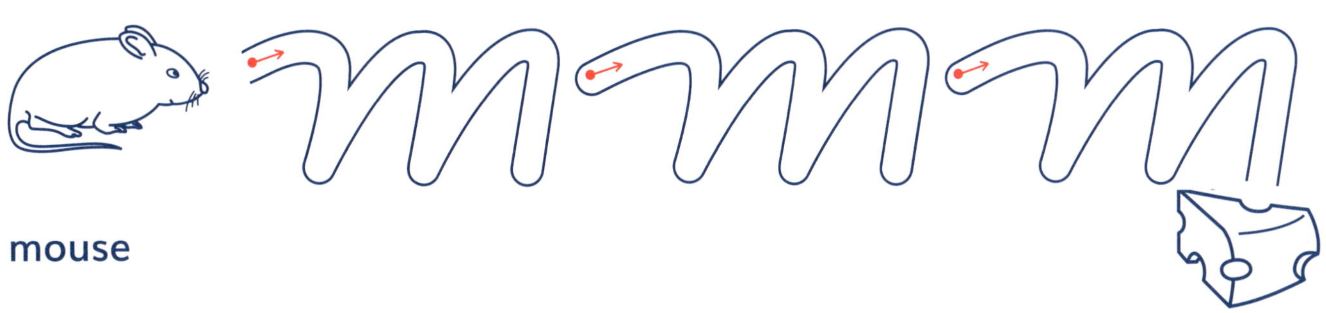

mouse

mountains

Trace the letter.

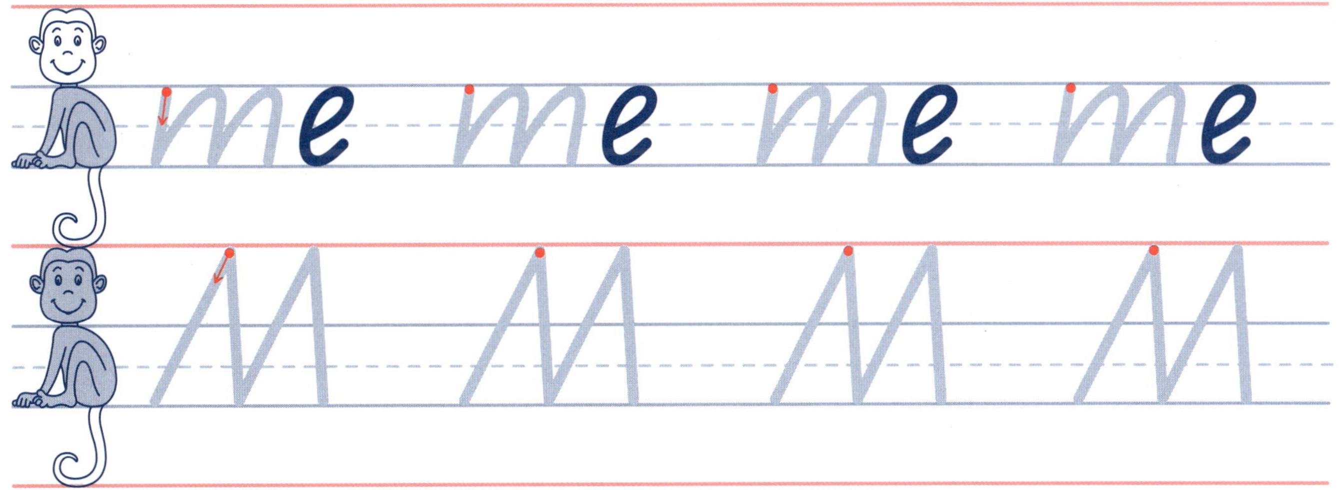

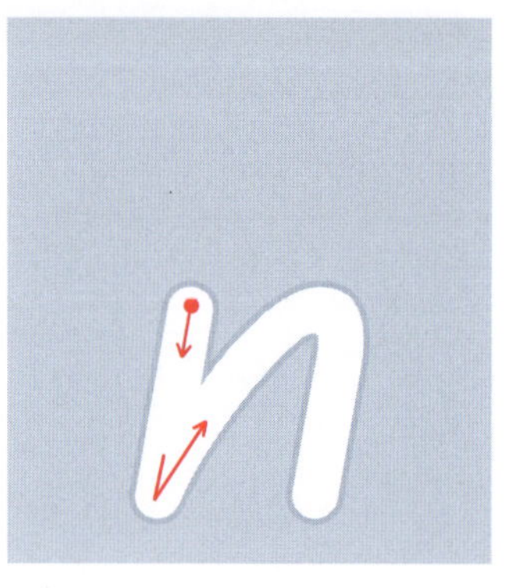

nose

Start at the red dot. Follow the arrow.

nest

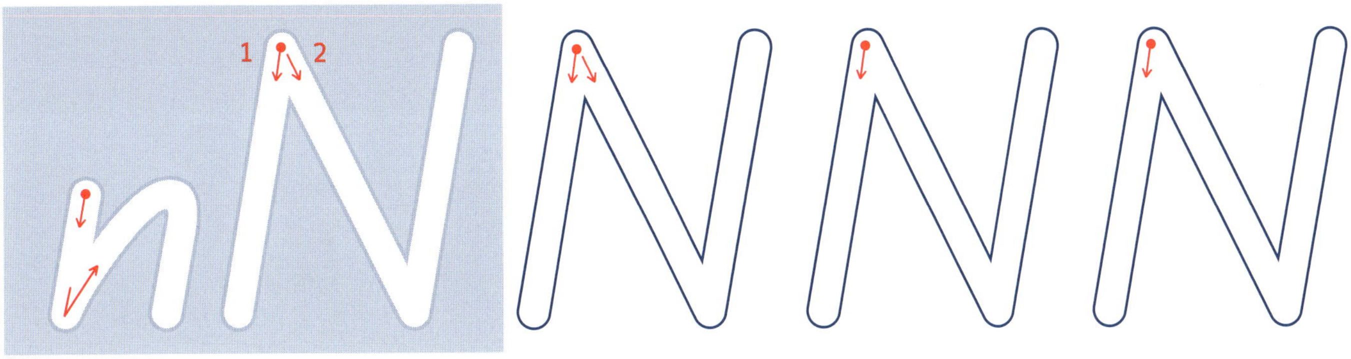

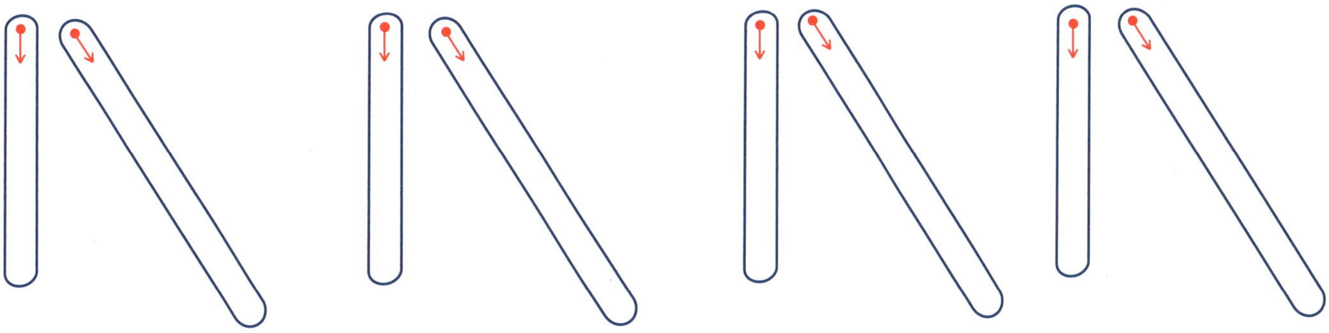

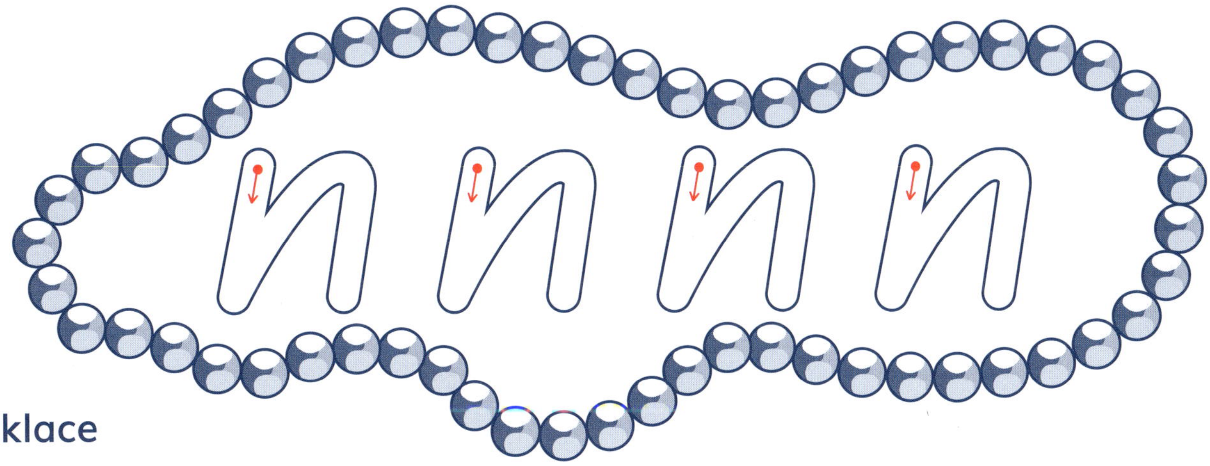

nN NNN

necklace

Trace the letter.

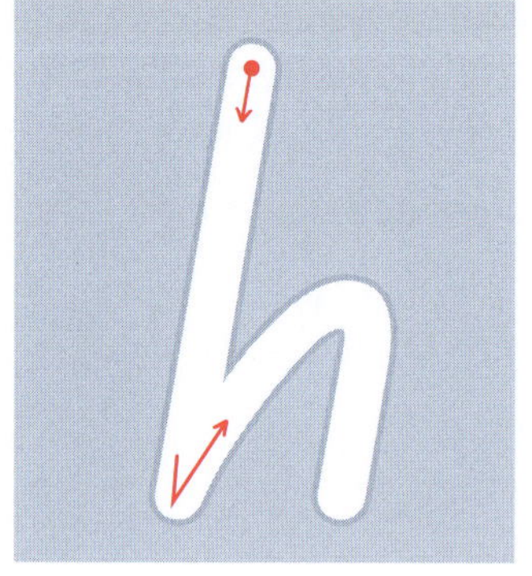

house

Start at the red dot. Follow the arrow.

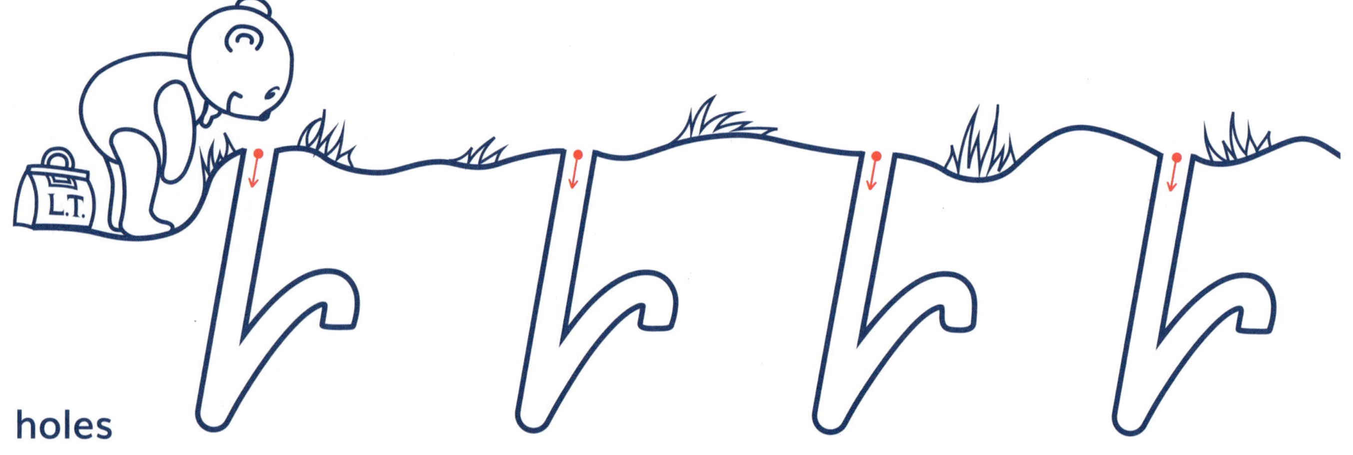

holes

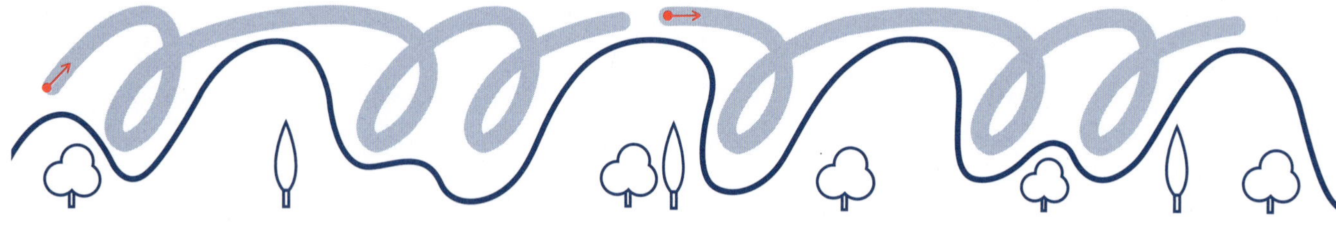

hills

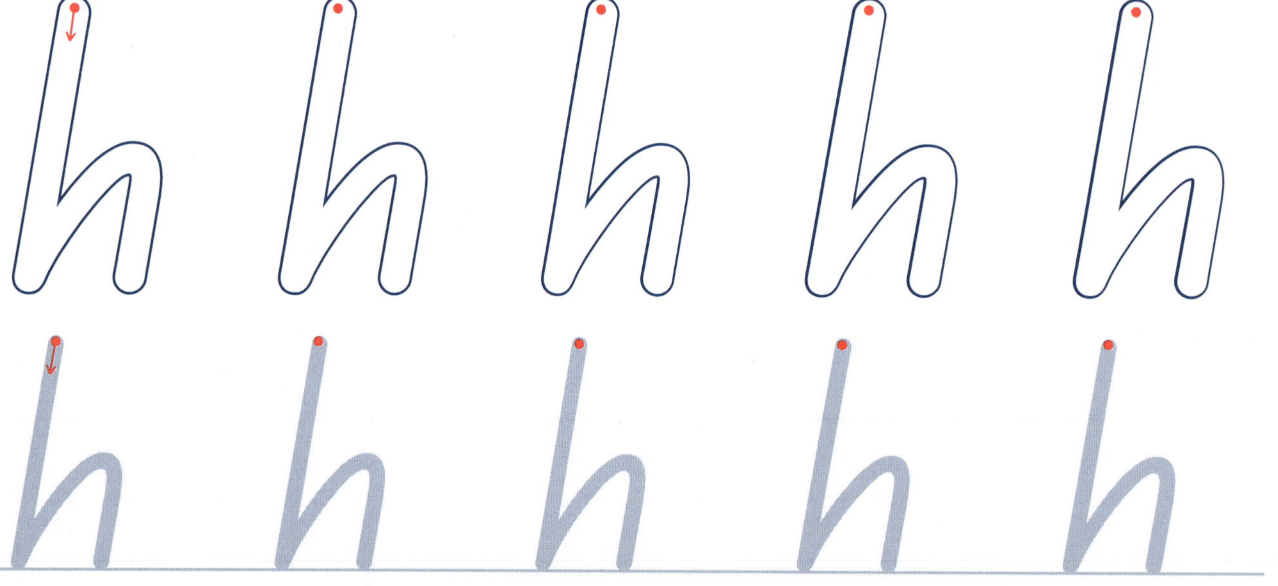

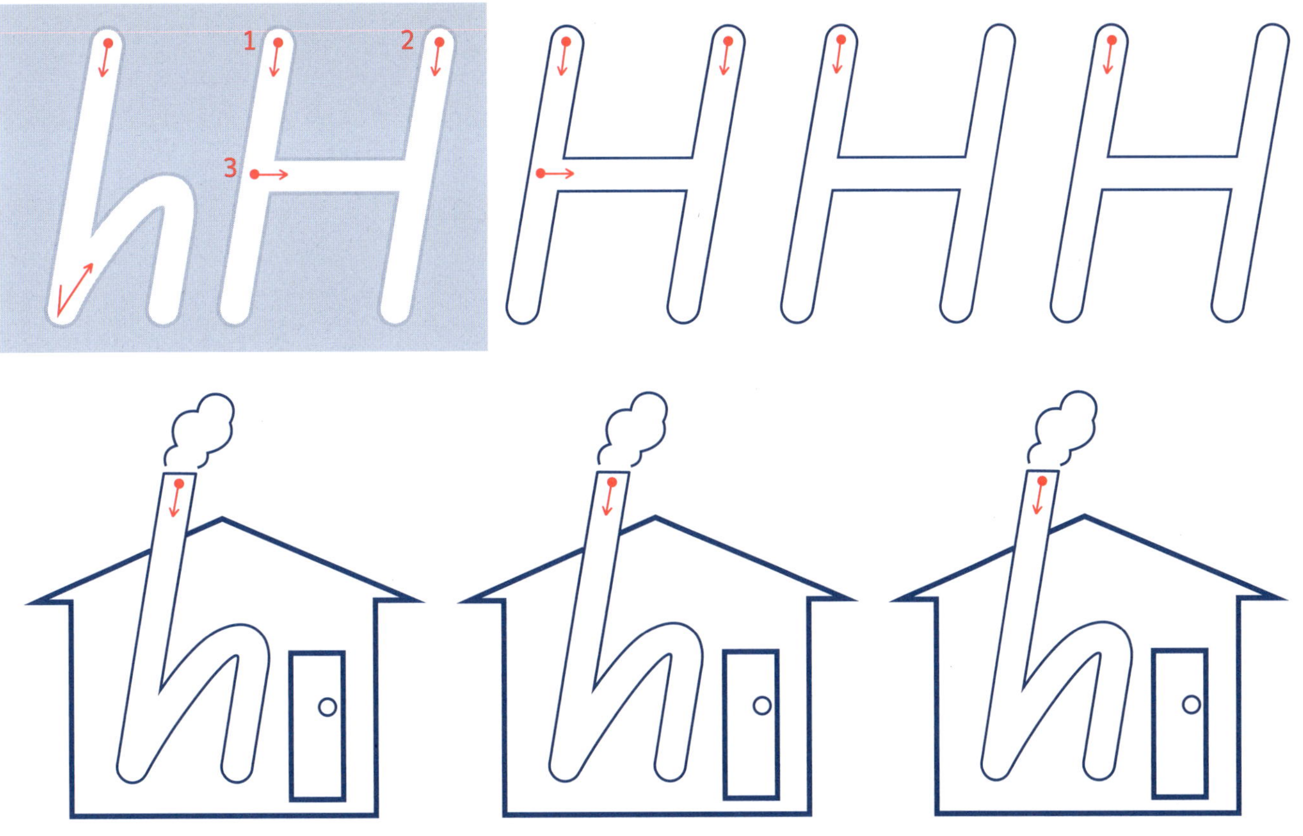

house

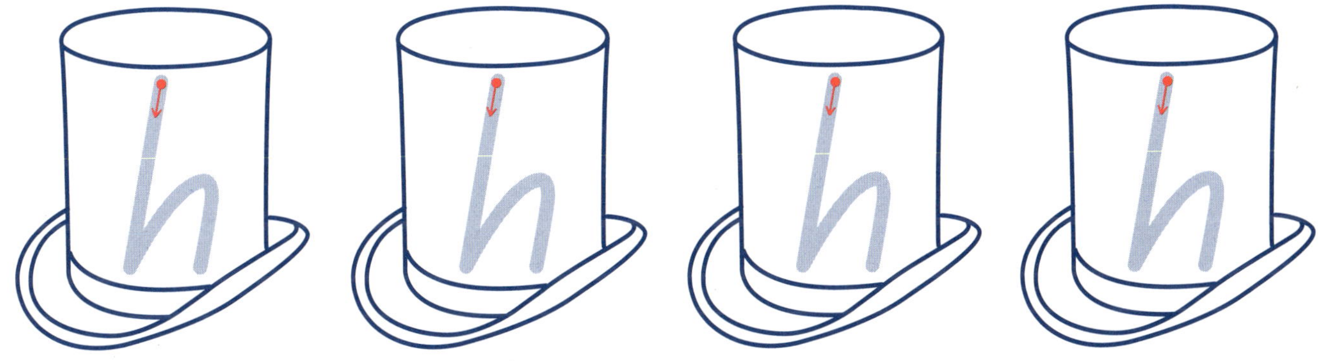

hat

Trace the letter.

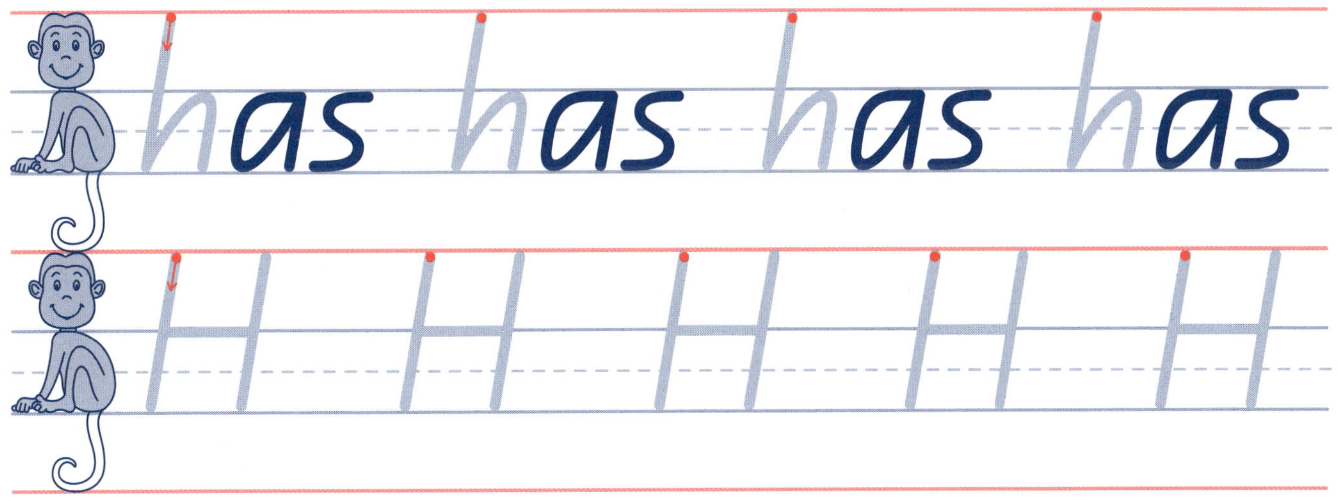

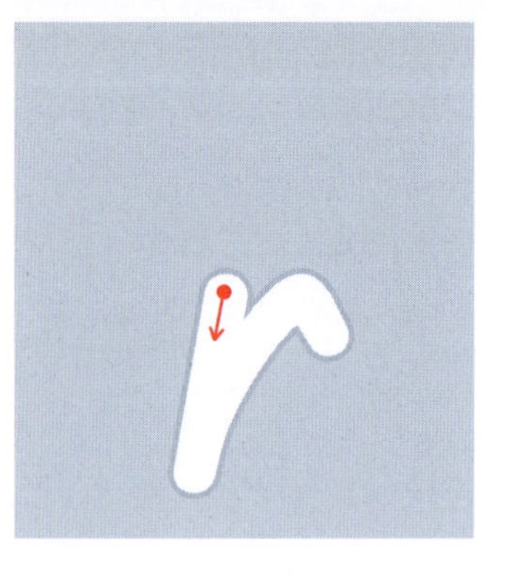

rain

Start at the red dot. Follow the arrow.

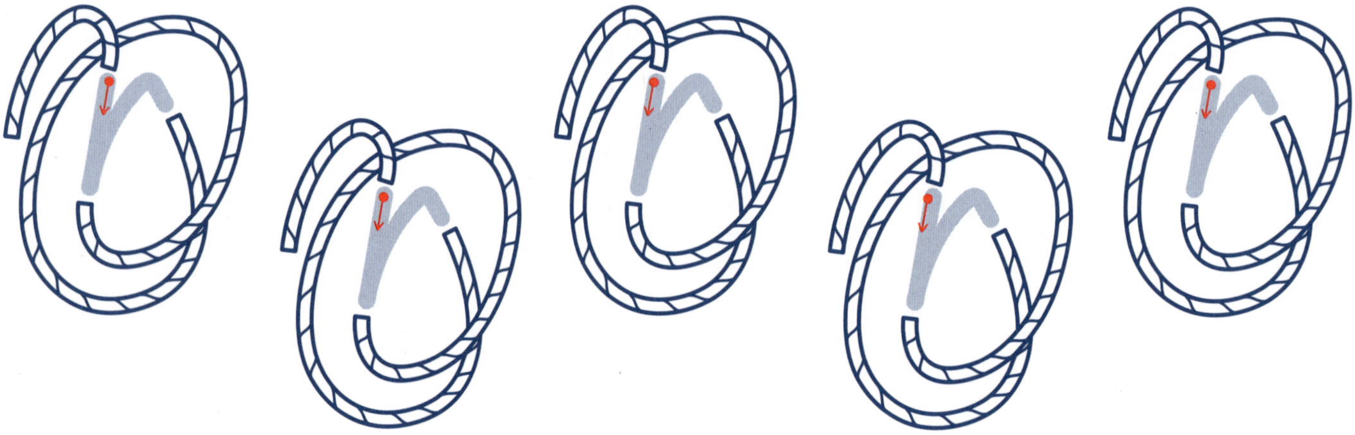

rope

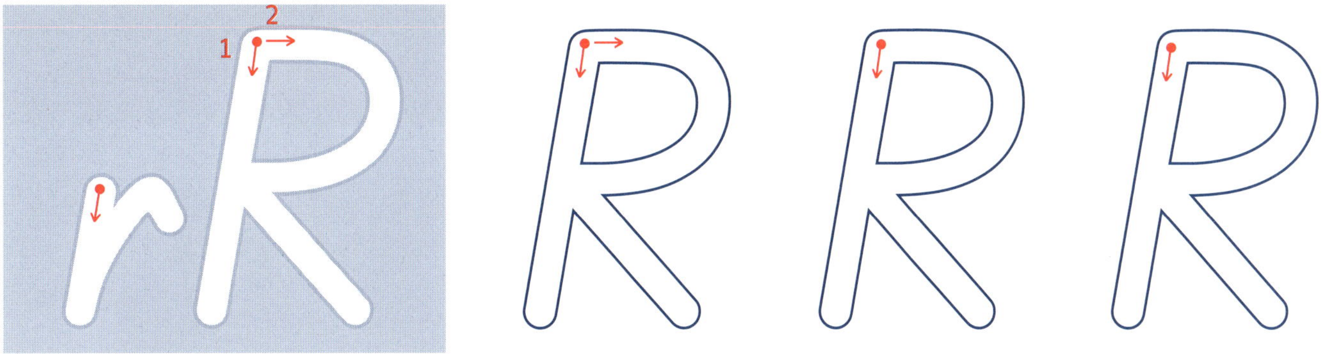

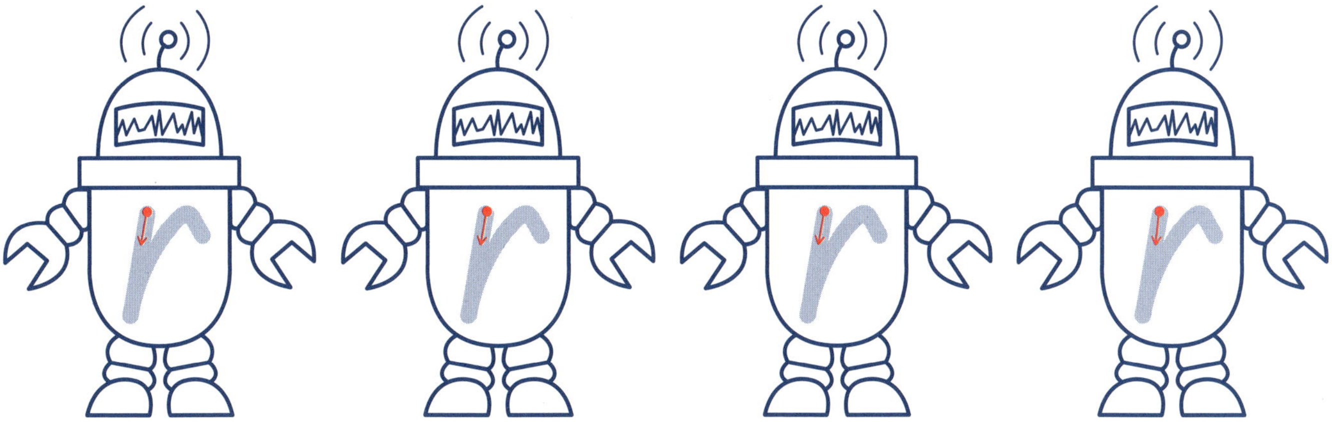

rR R R R

robot

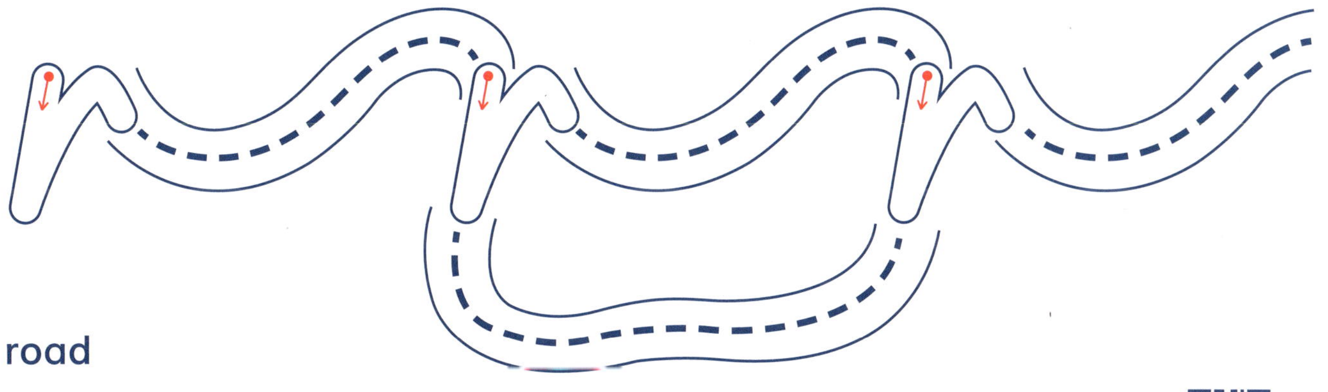

road

get.ga/PMWA2

Trace the letter.

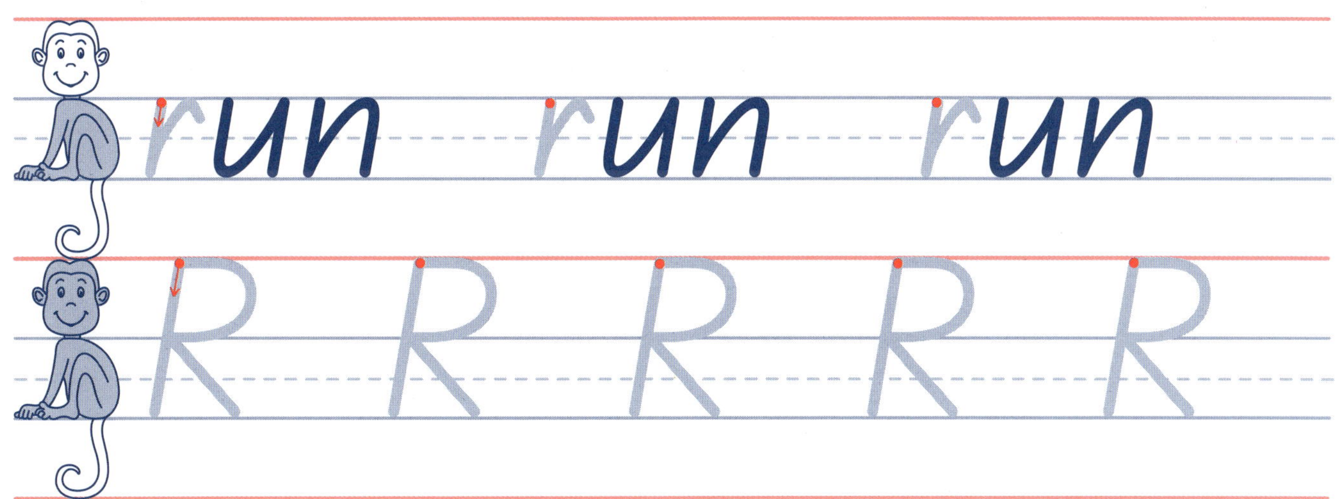

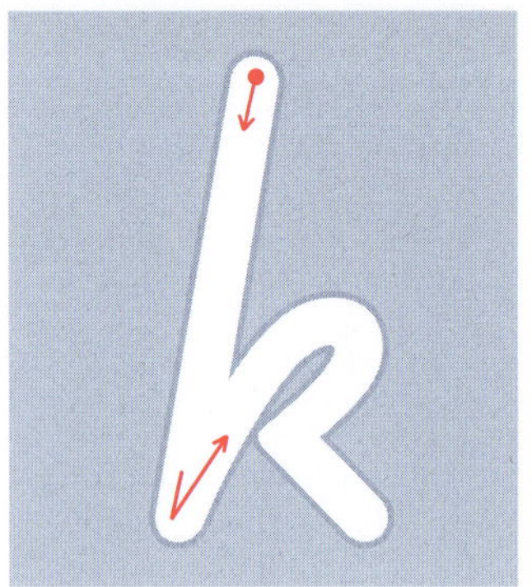

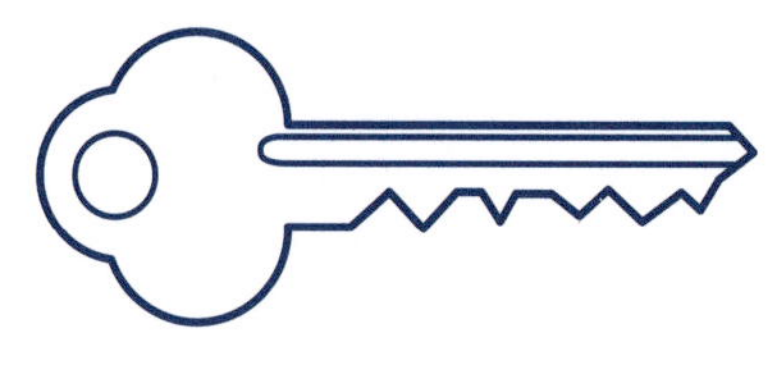

key

Start at the red dot. Follow the arrow.

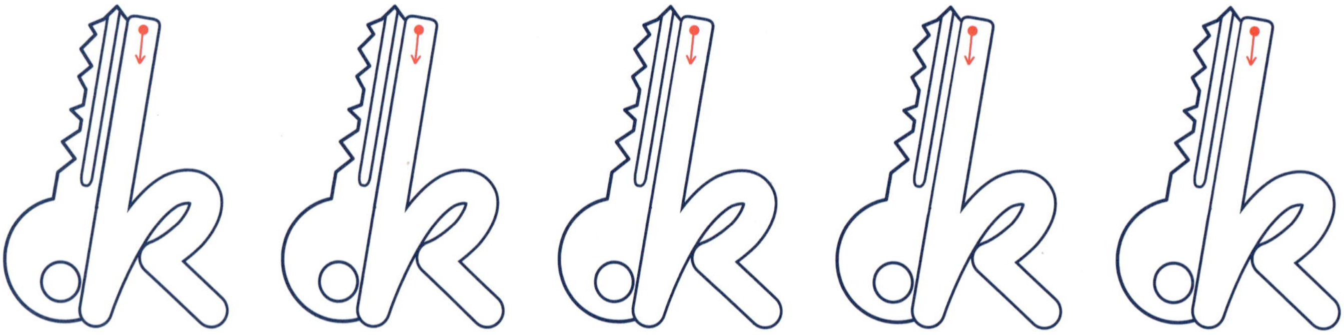

key

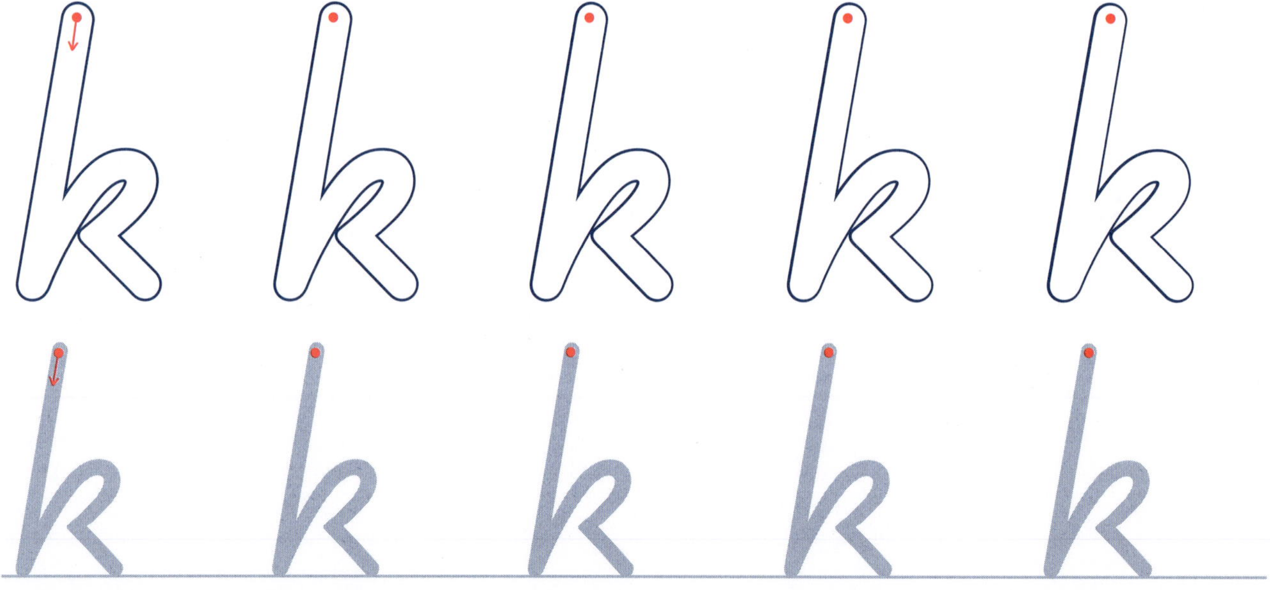

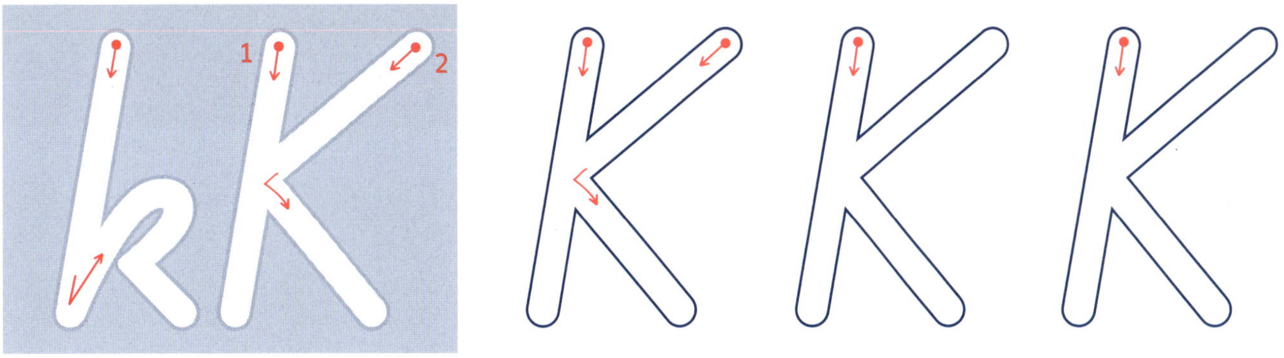

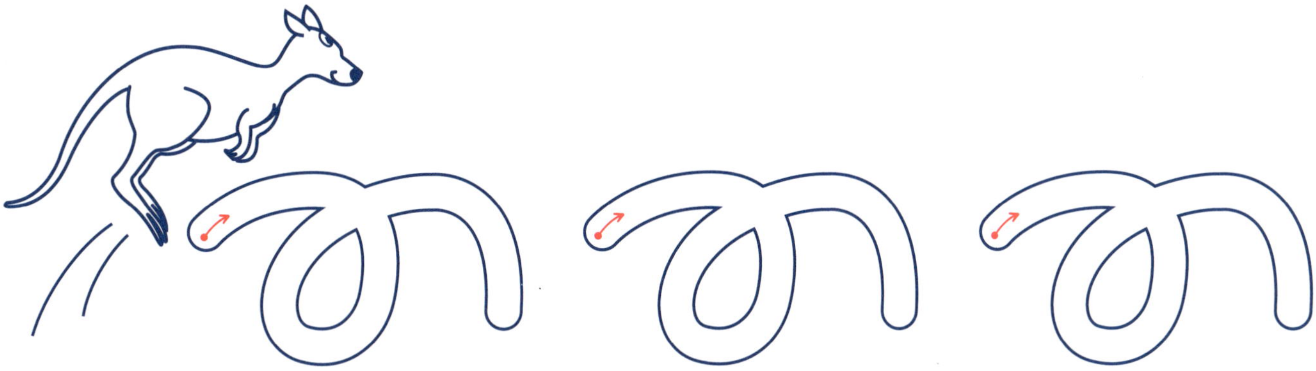

kangaroo

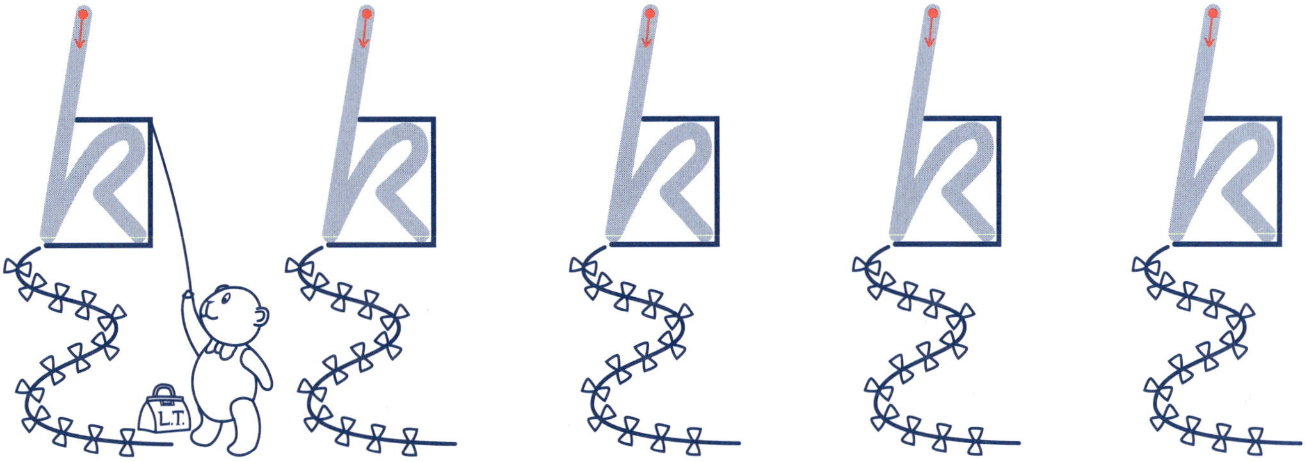

kite

Trace the letter.

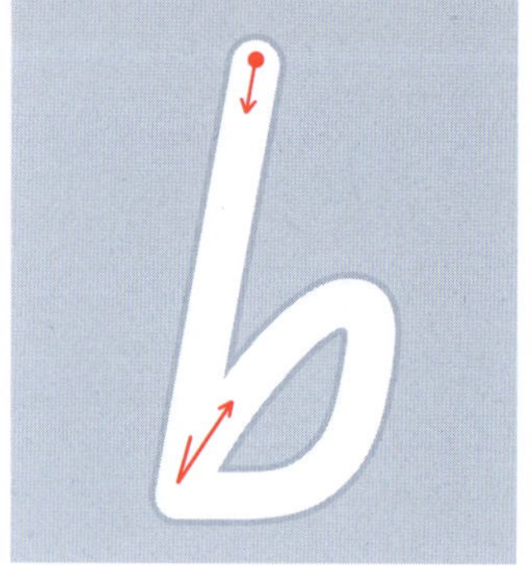

balloons

Start at the red dot. Follow the arrow.

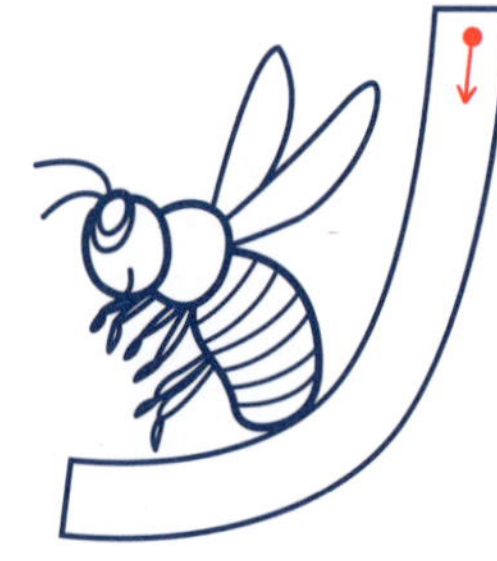

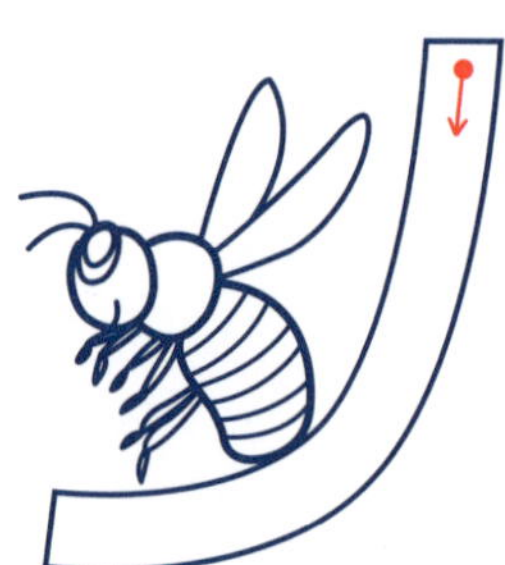

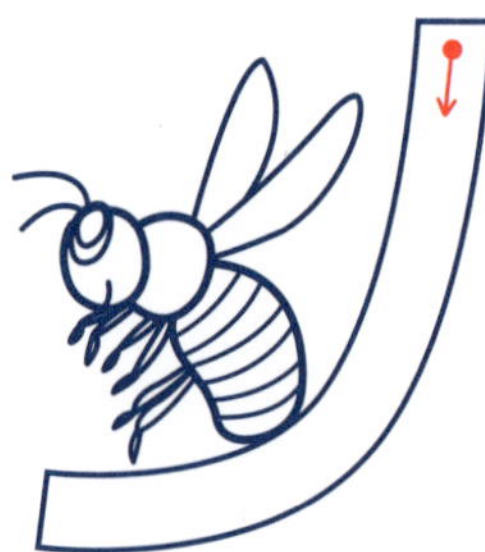

bee

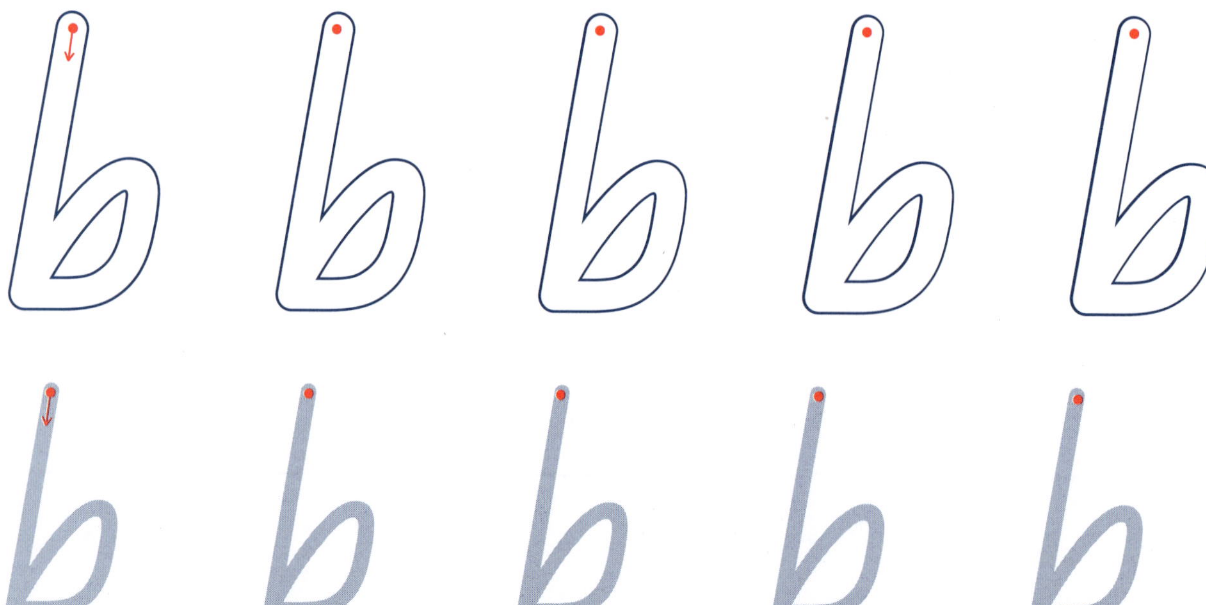

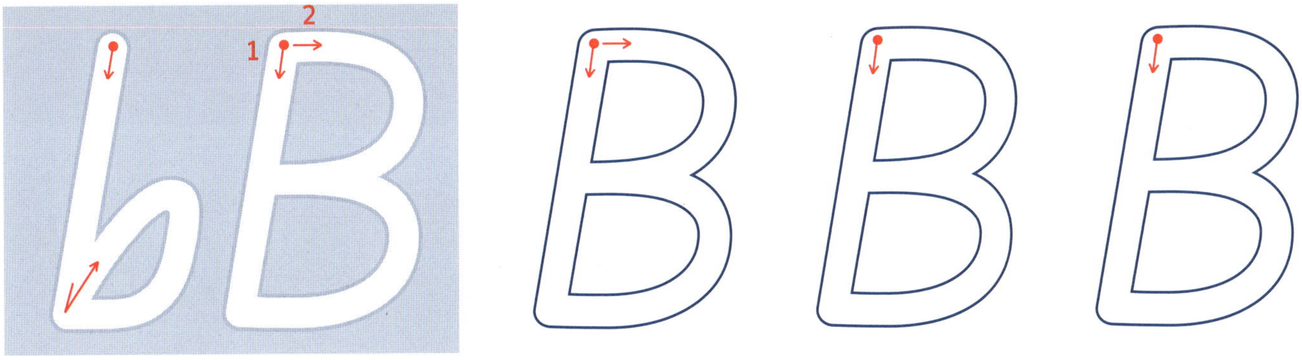

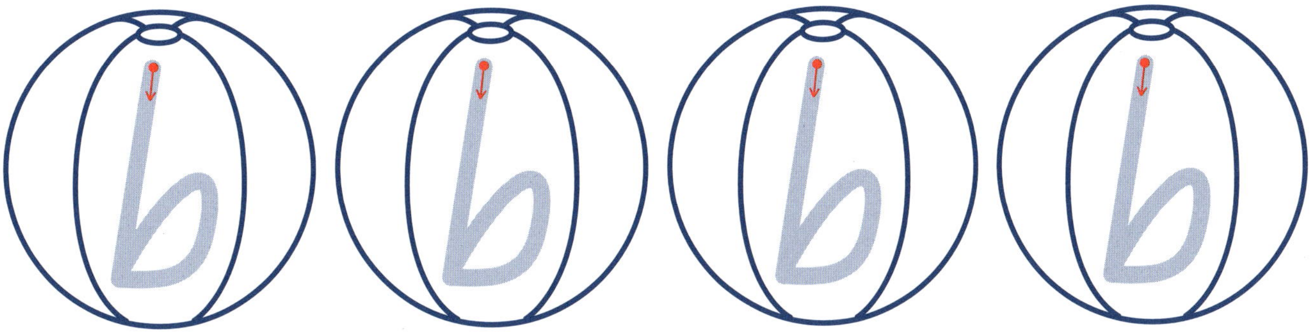

bB B B B

ball

boat

Trace the letter.

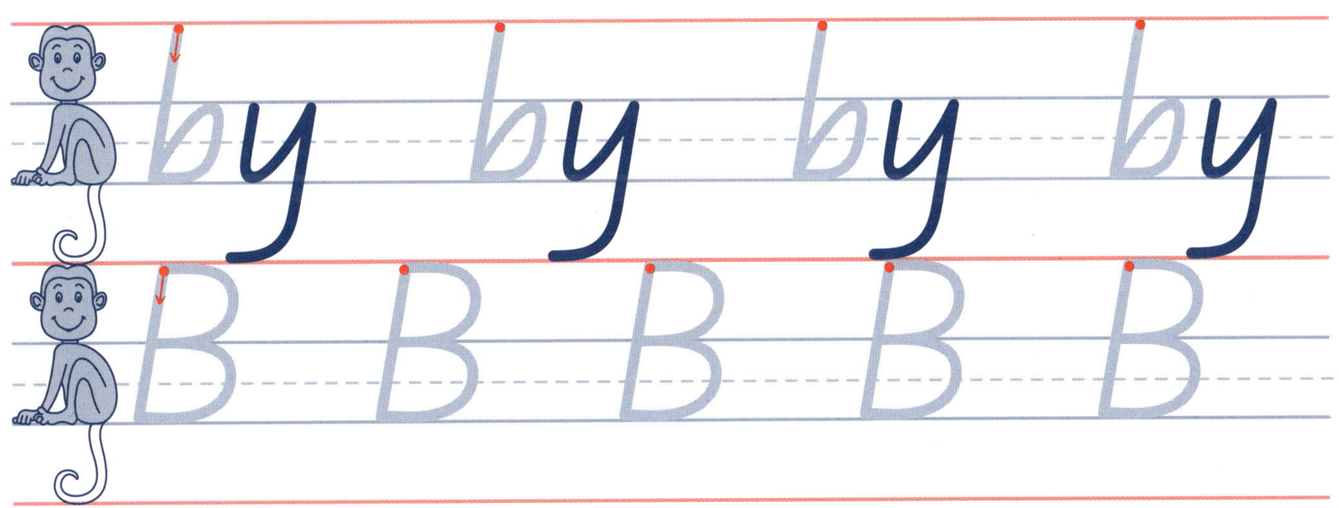

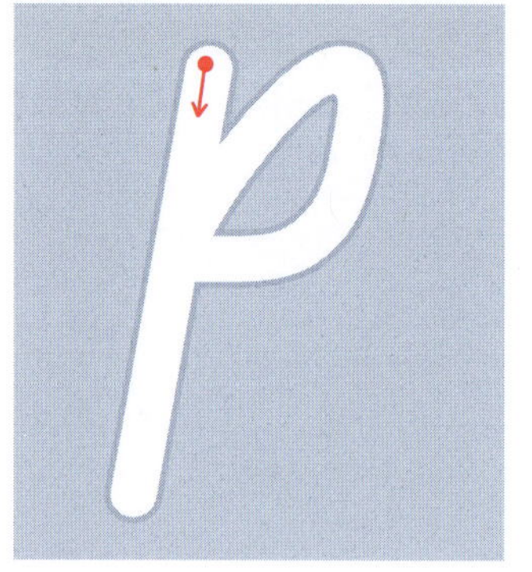

paint

Start at the red dot. Follow the arrow.

pencil

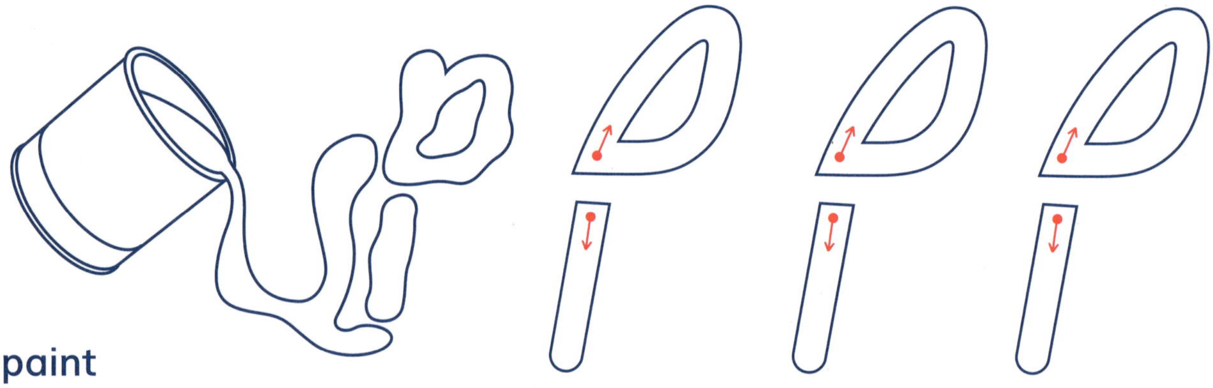

paint

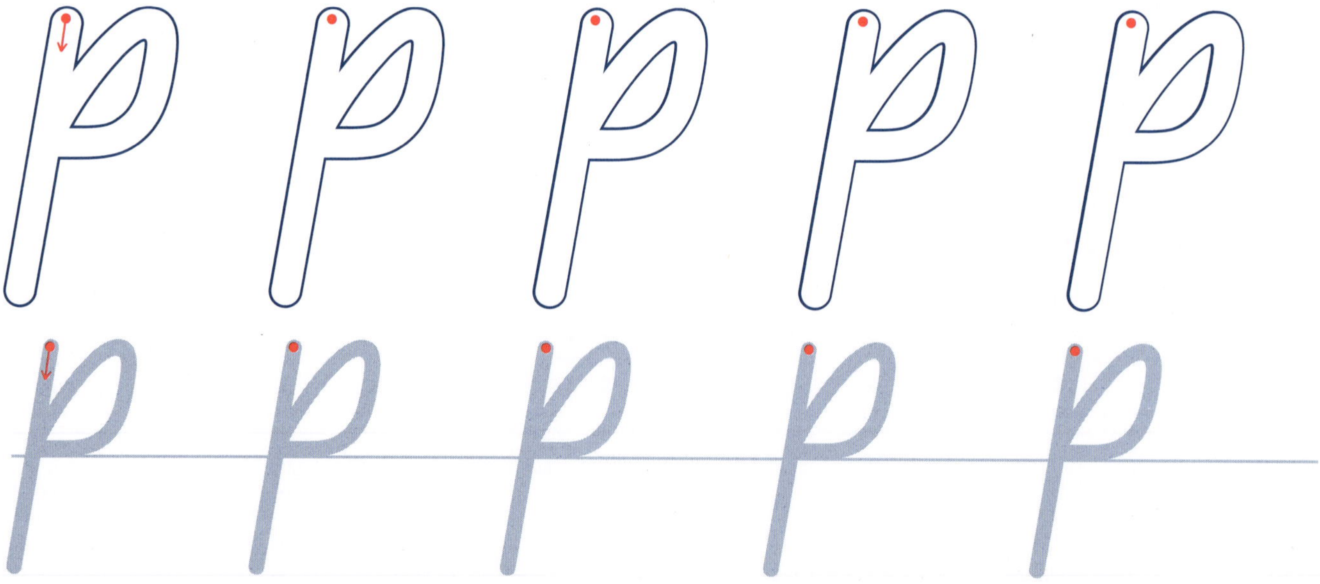

pP

1 2

P P P

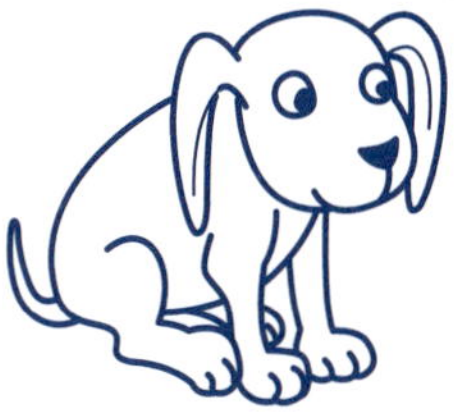

puppy

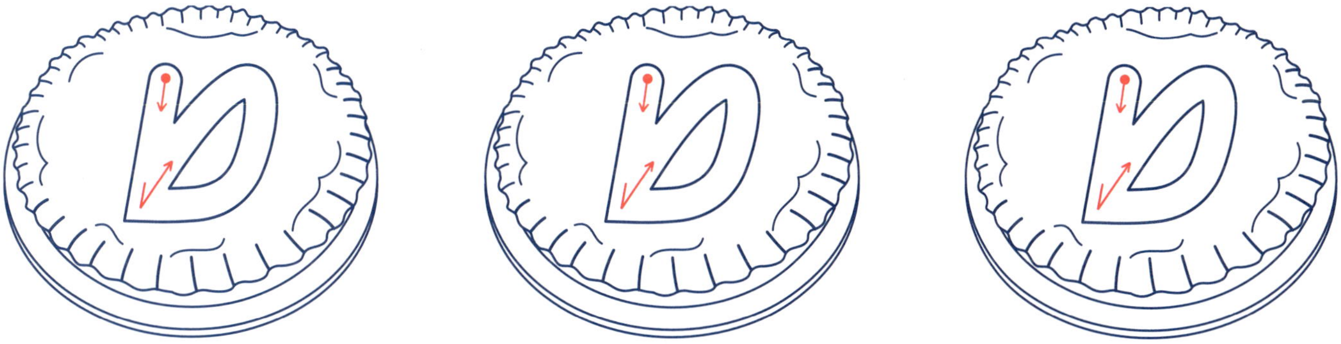

pie

Trace the letter.

play play play

P P P P P

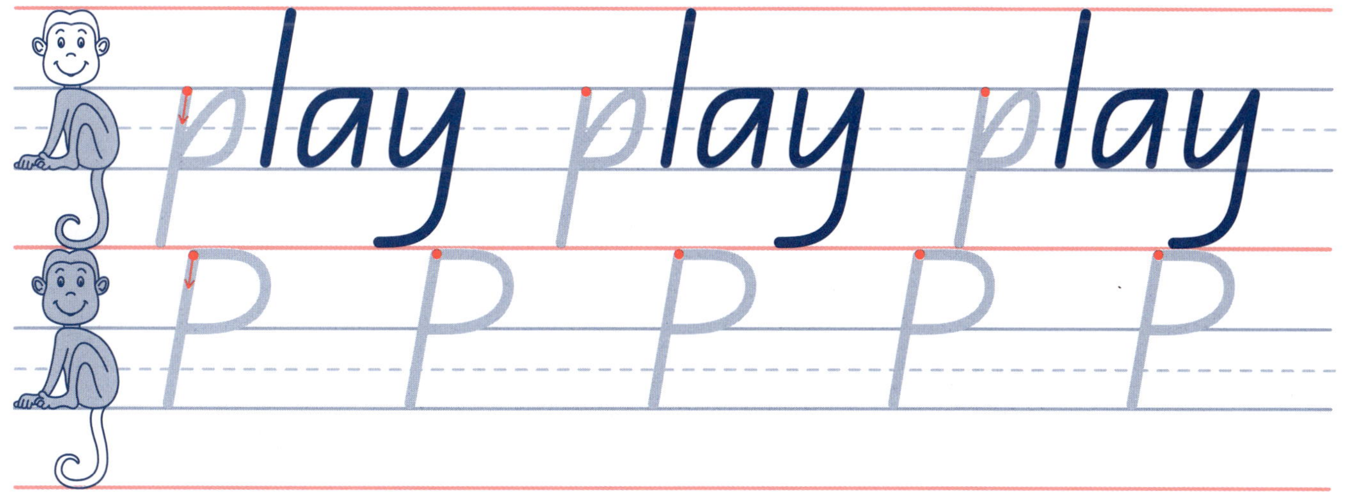

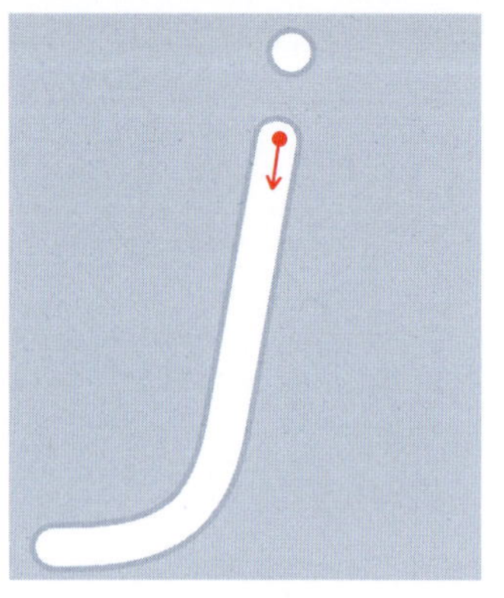

jam

Start at the red dot. Follow the arrow.

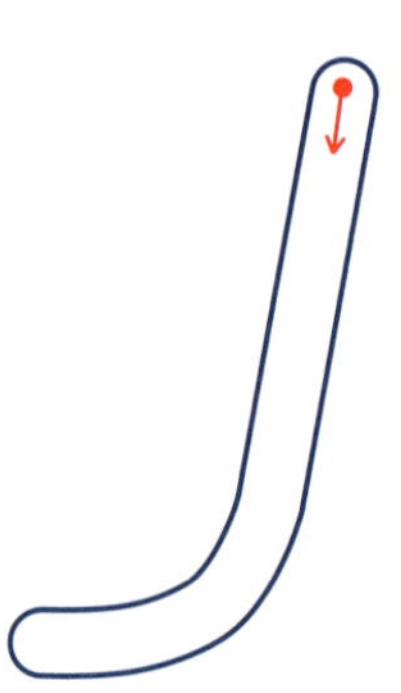

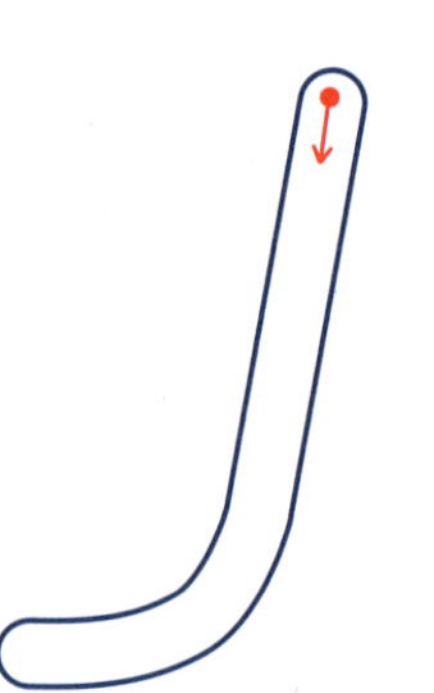

jump

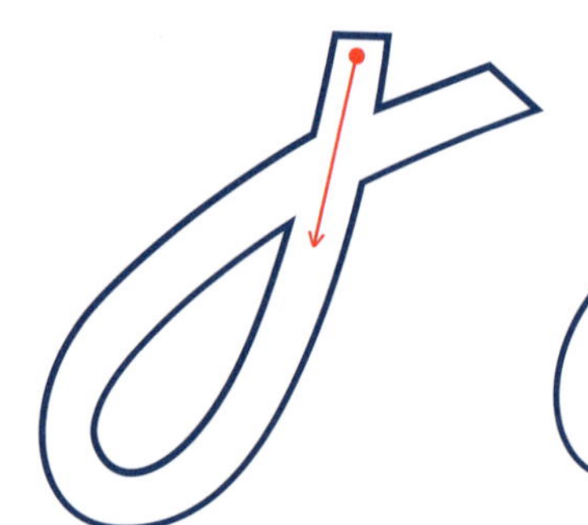

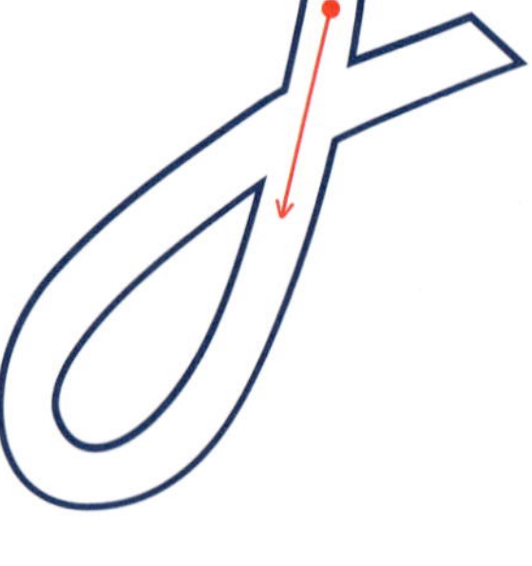

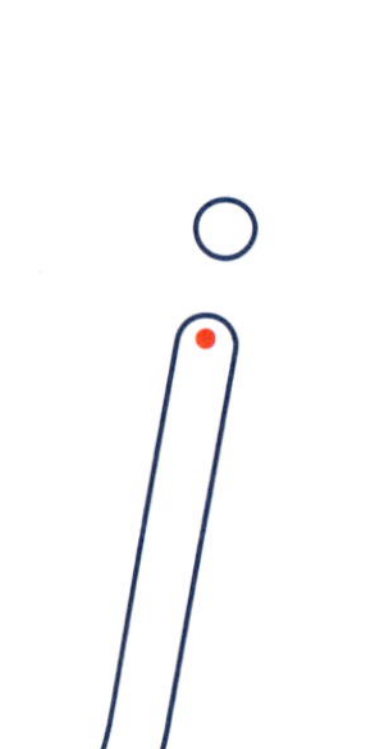

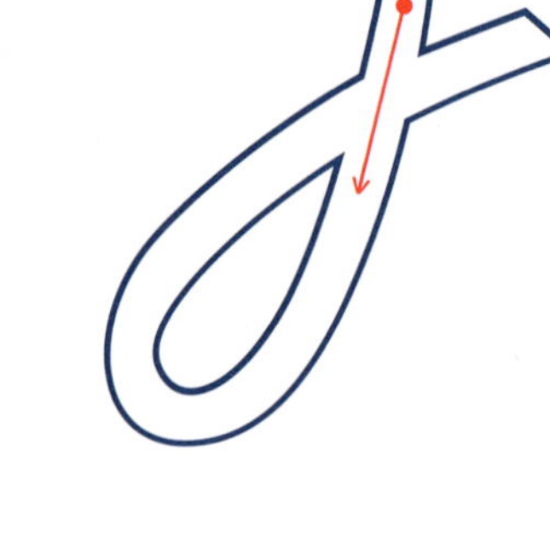

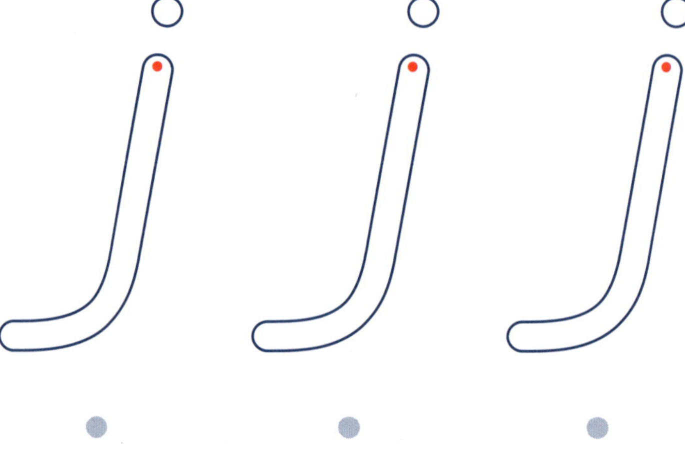

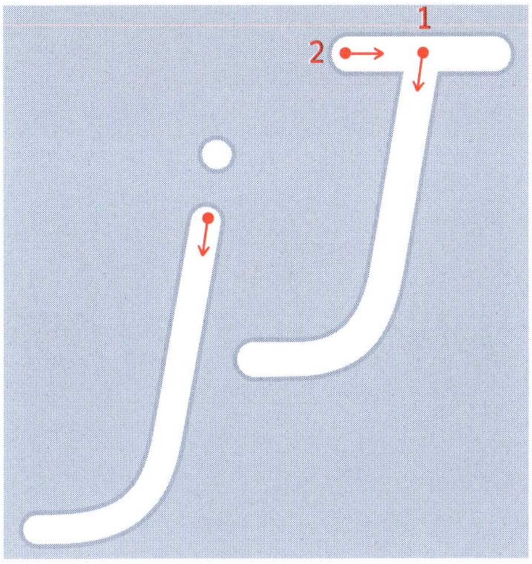

1
2

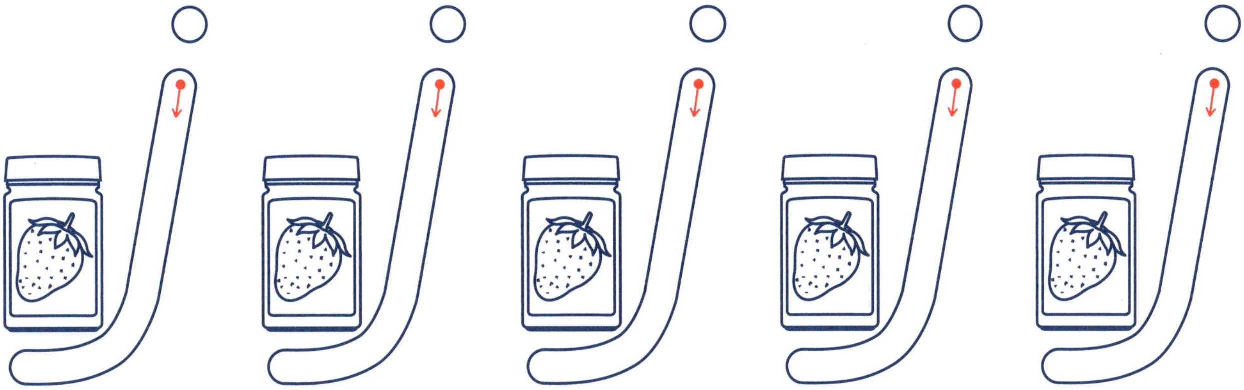

jam

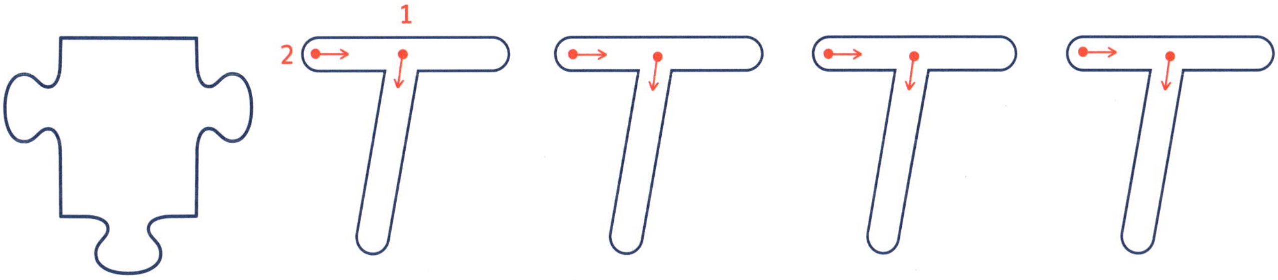

1
2

jigsaw

get.ga/PMWA3

Trace the letter.

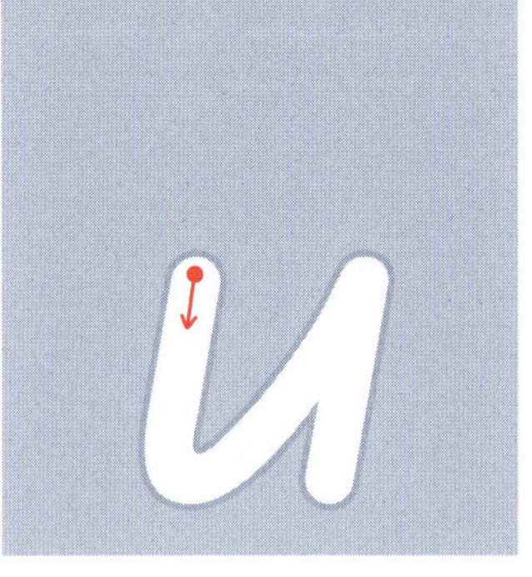

umbrella

Start at the red dot. Follow the arrow.

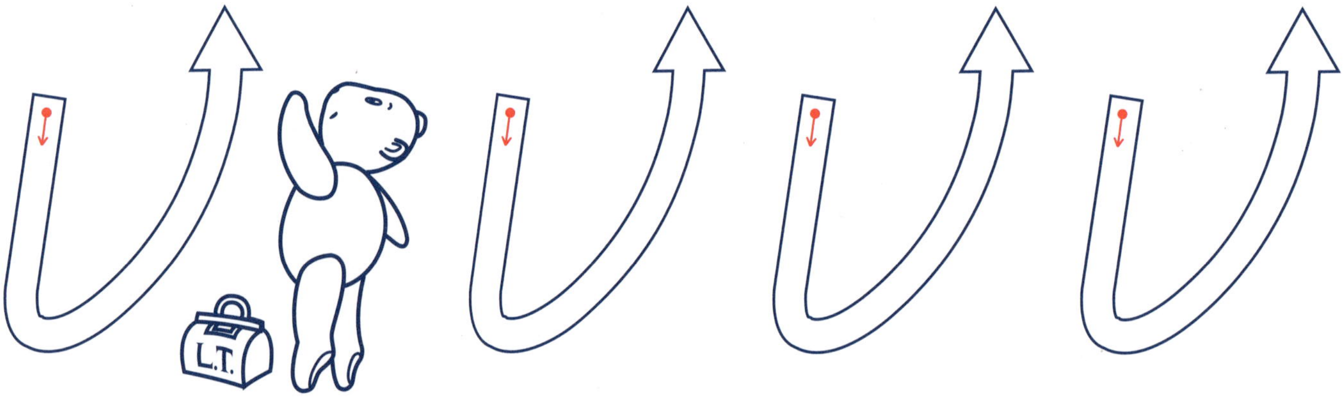

up

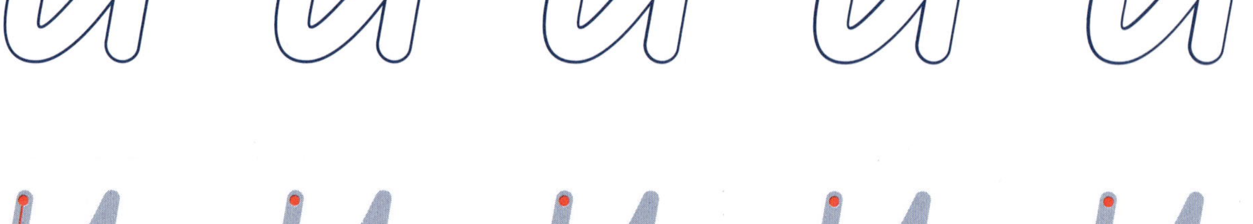

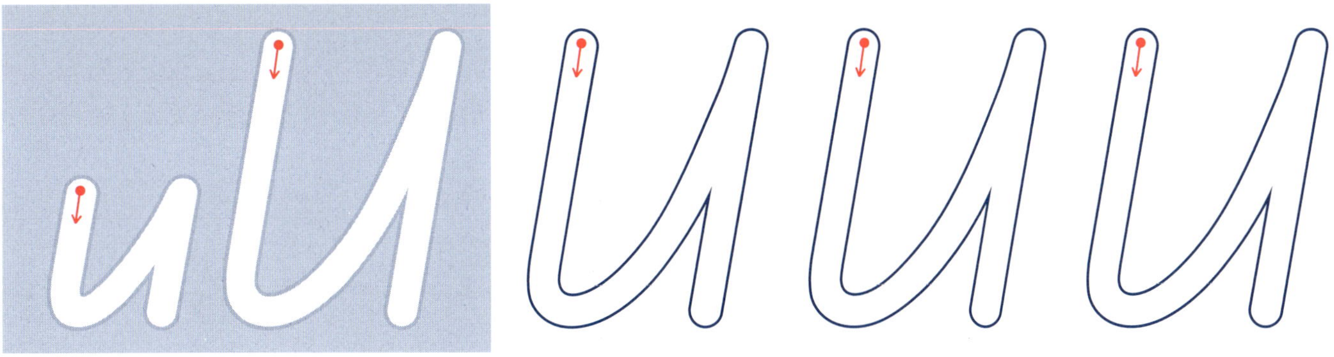

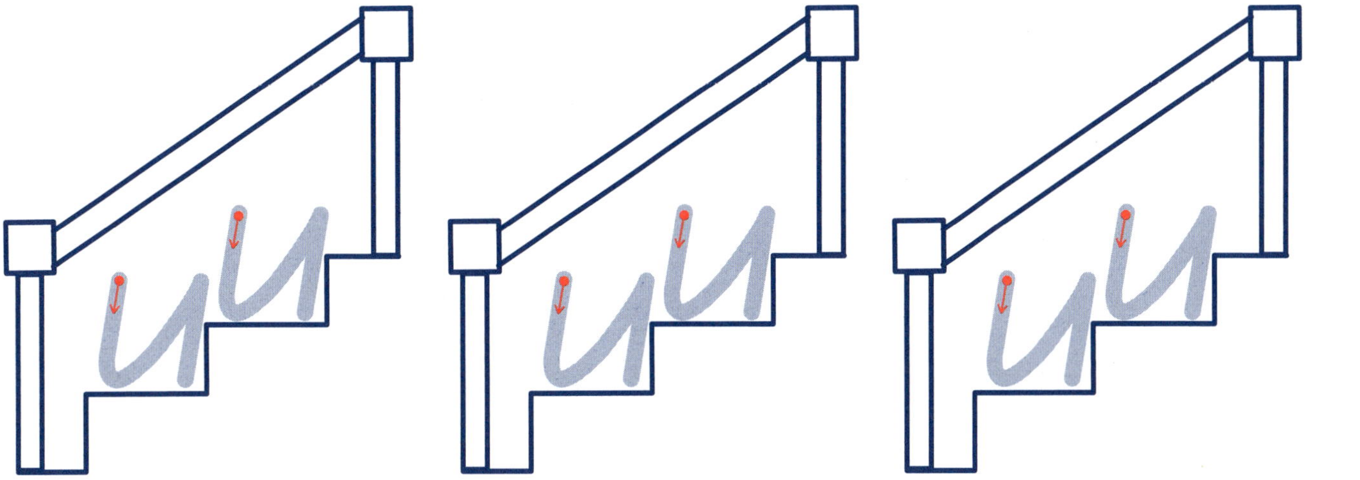

upstairs

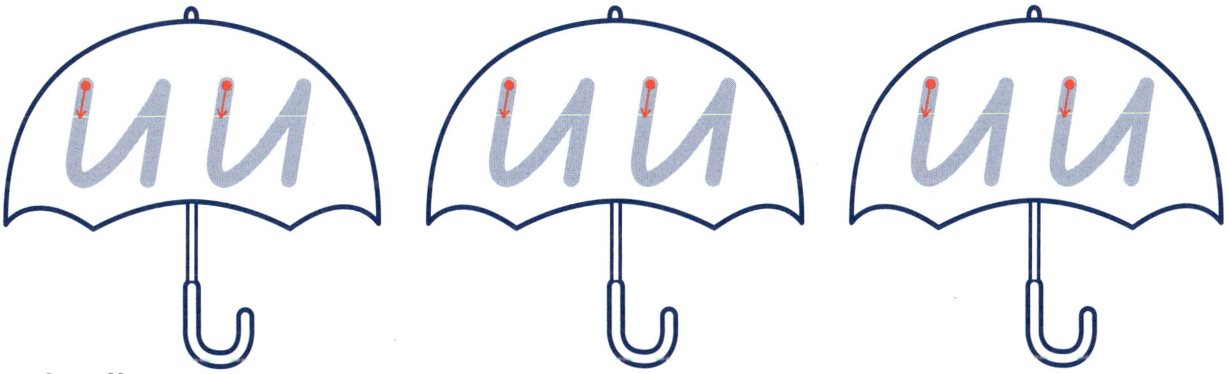

umbrella

Trace the letter.

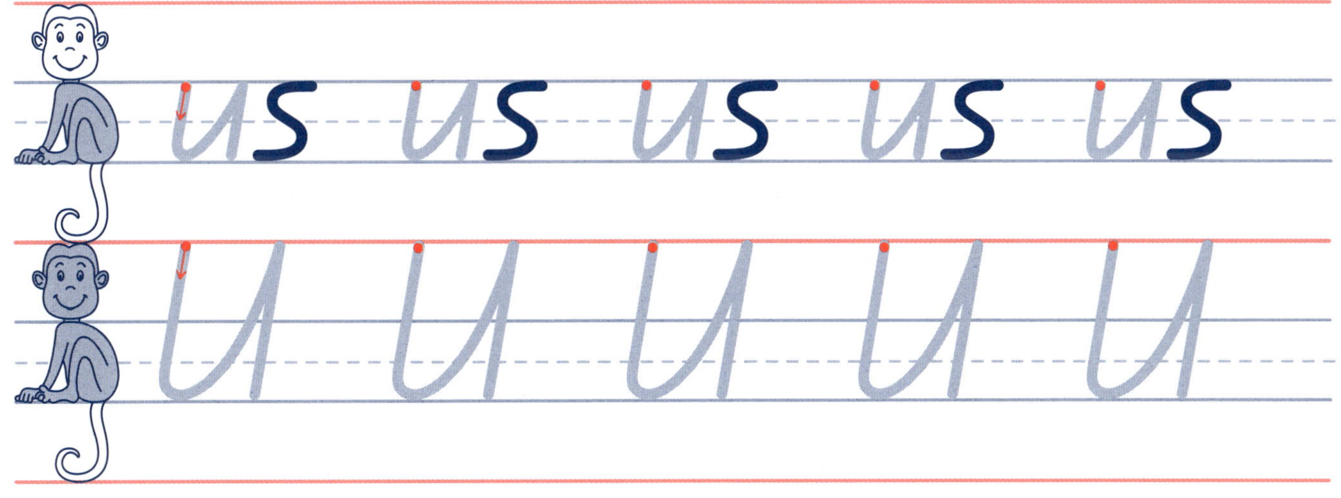

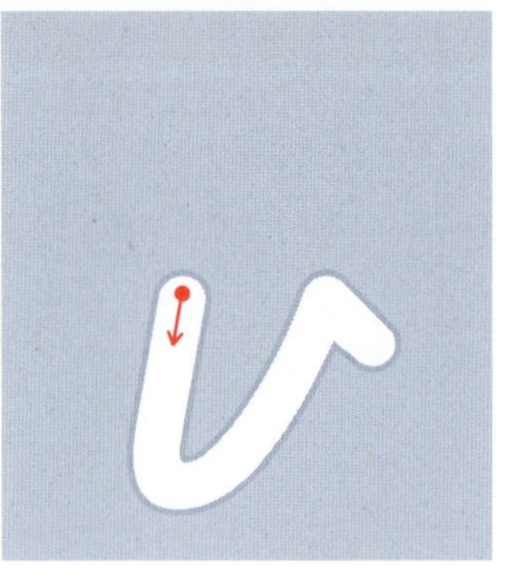

van

Start at the red dot. Follow the arrow.

volcano

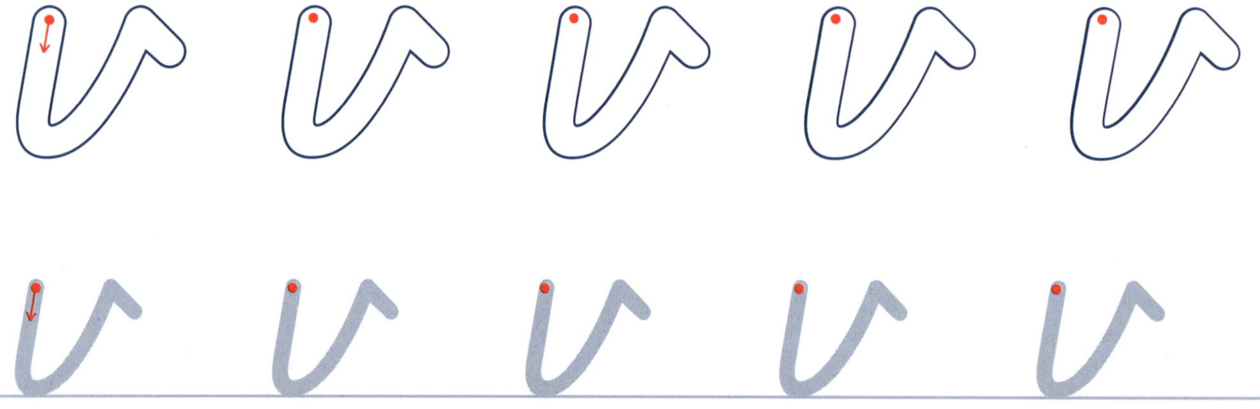

van

vase

Trace the letter.

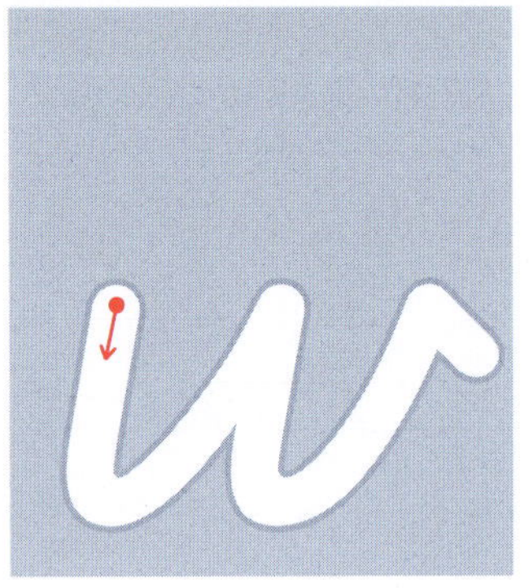

window

Start at the red dot. Follow the arrow.

waves

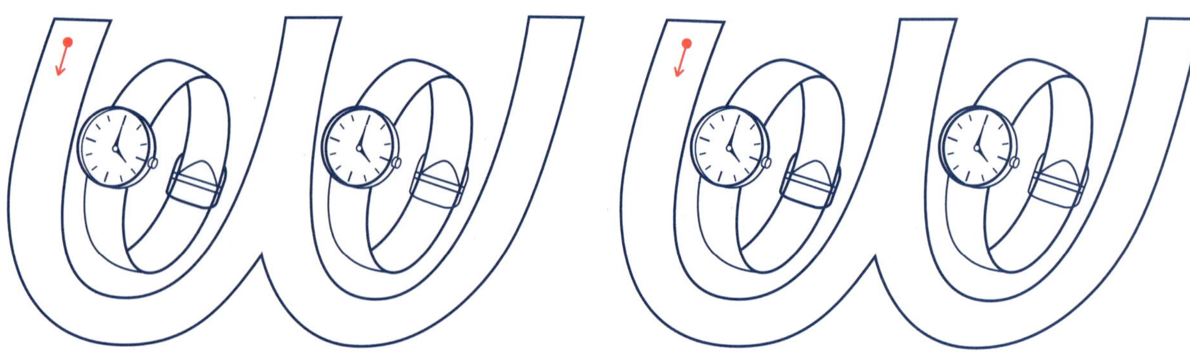

watches

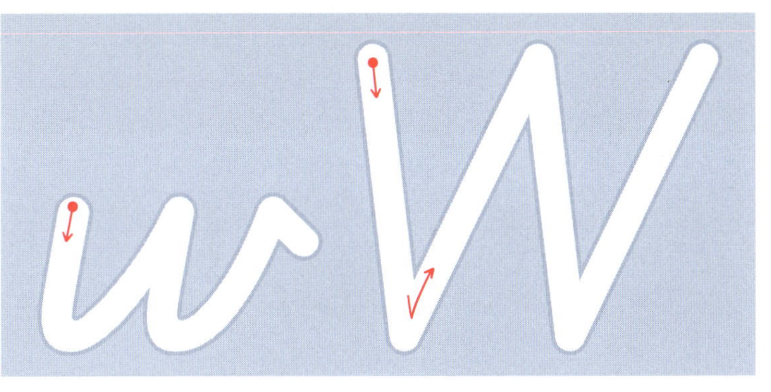

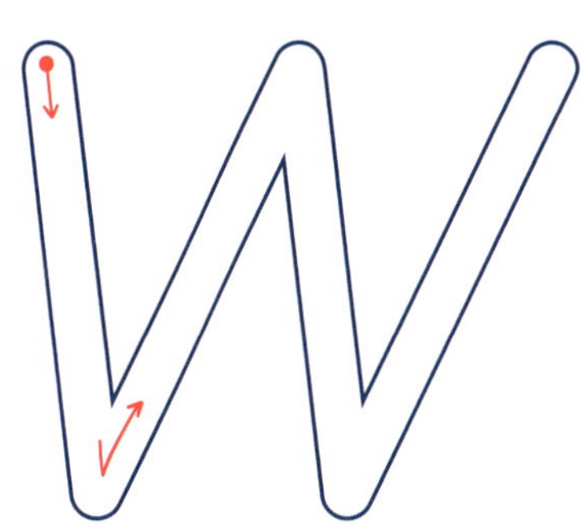

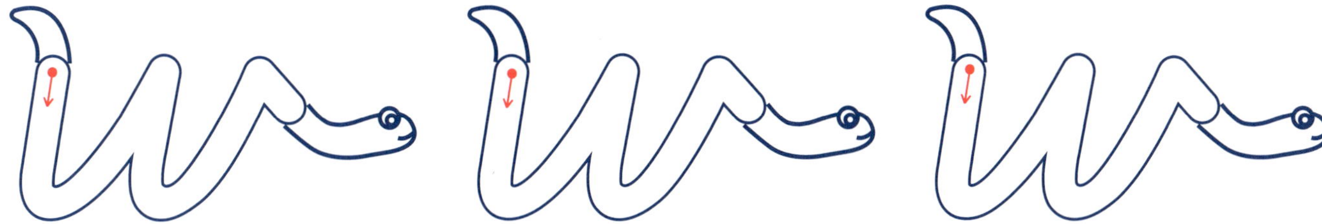

worm

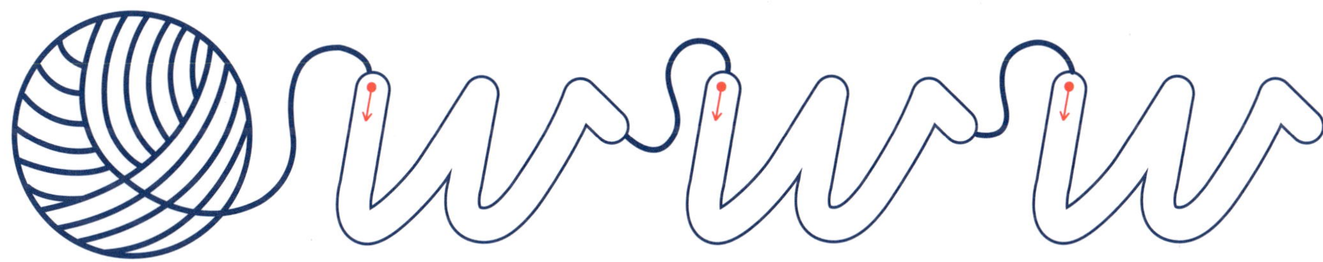

wool

Trace the letter.

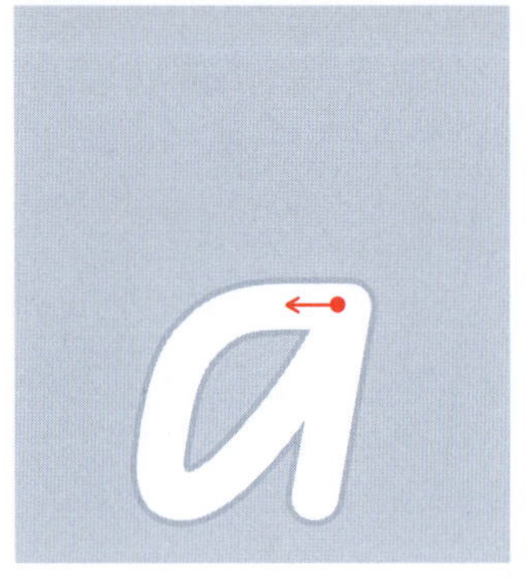

apple

Start at the red dot. Follow the arrow.

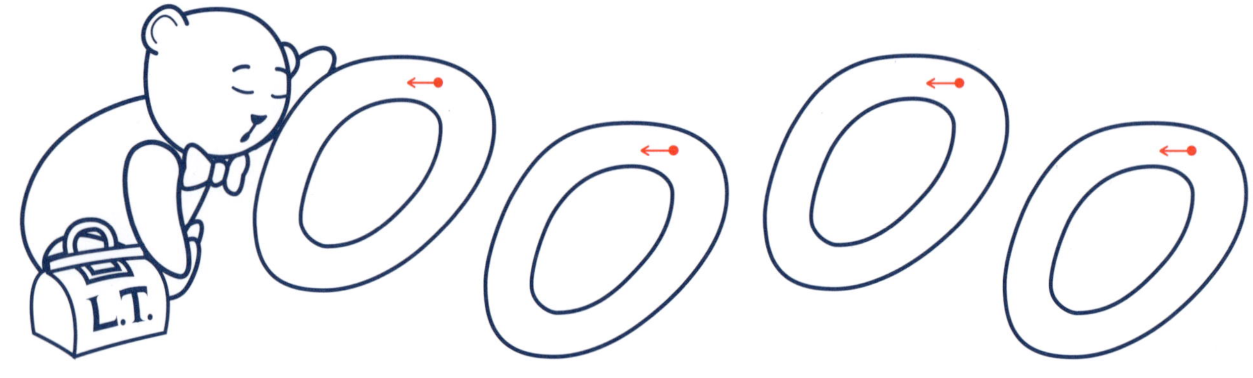

asleep

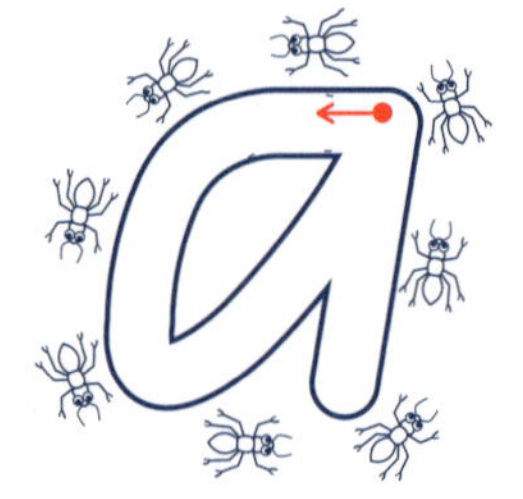
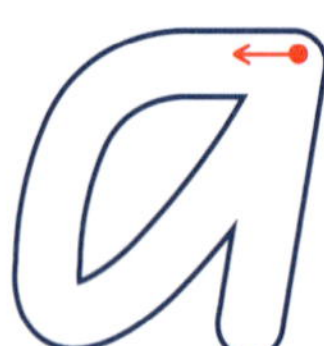

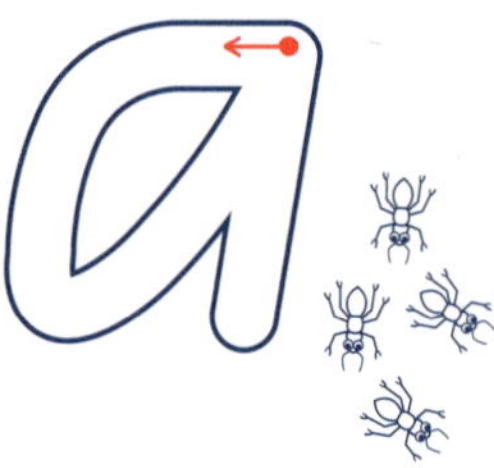

ants

aA

1 2 3

AAA

apple

Trace the letter.

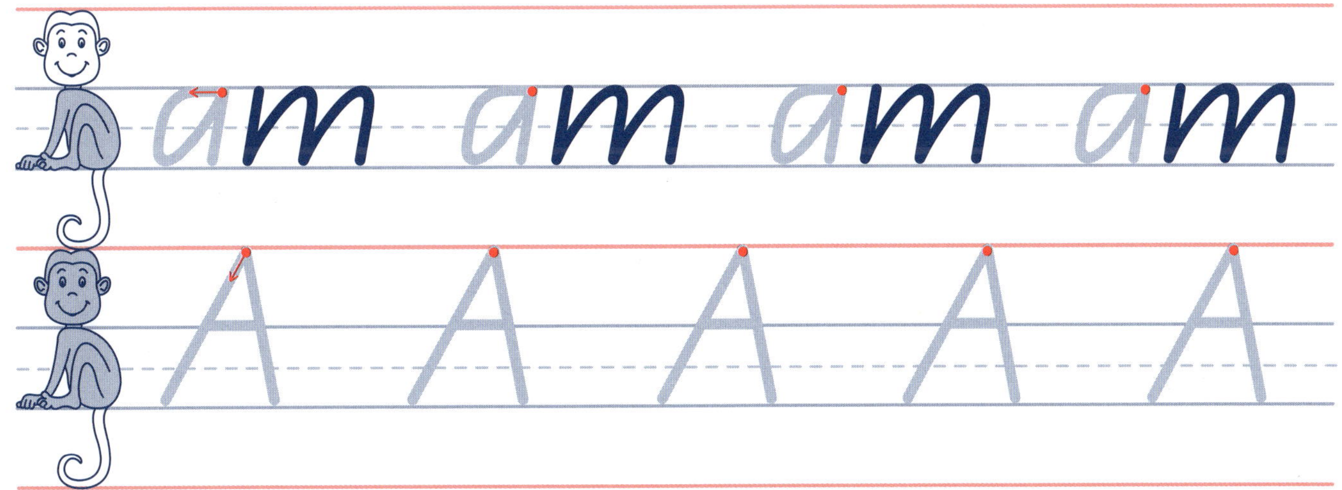

caterpillar

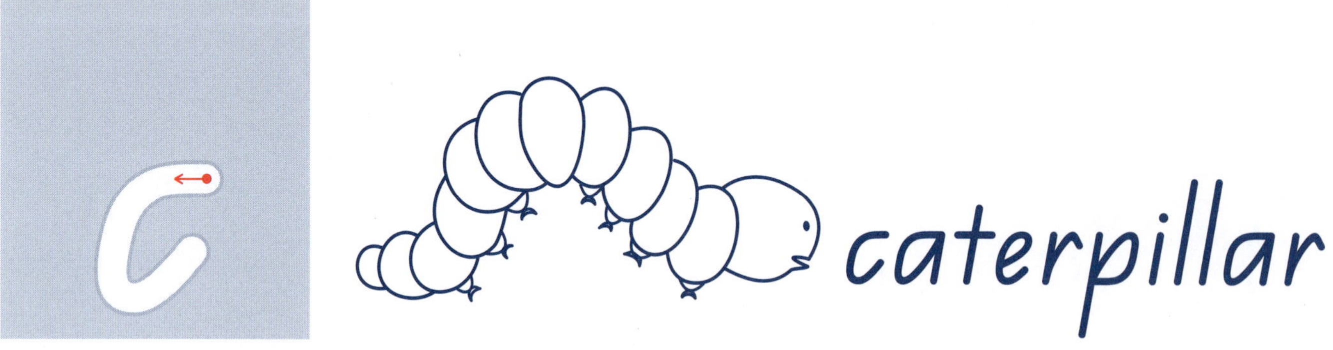

Start at the red dot. Follow the arrow.

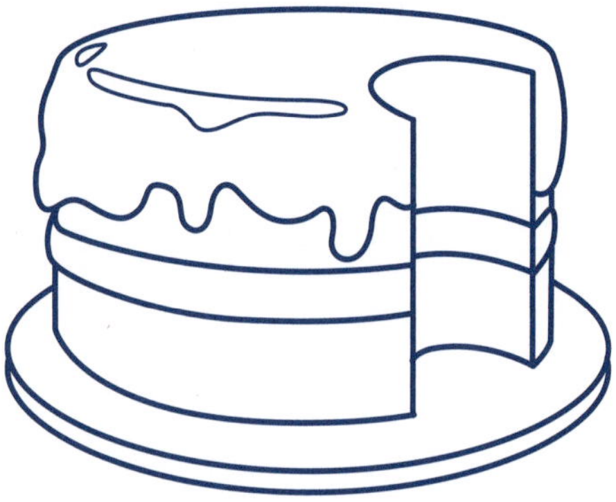

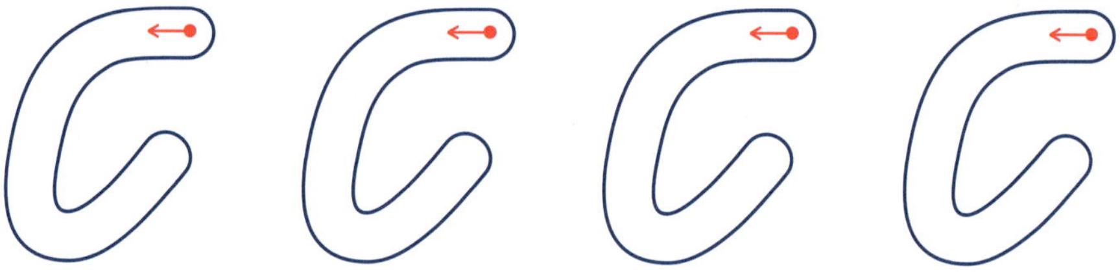

cake

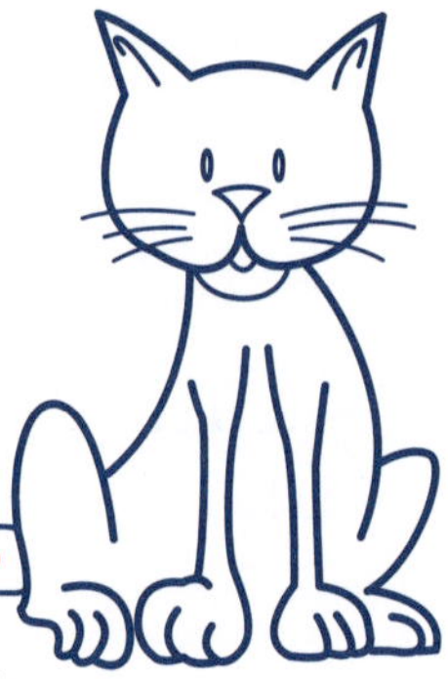

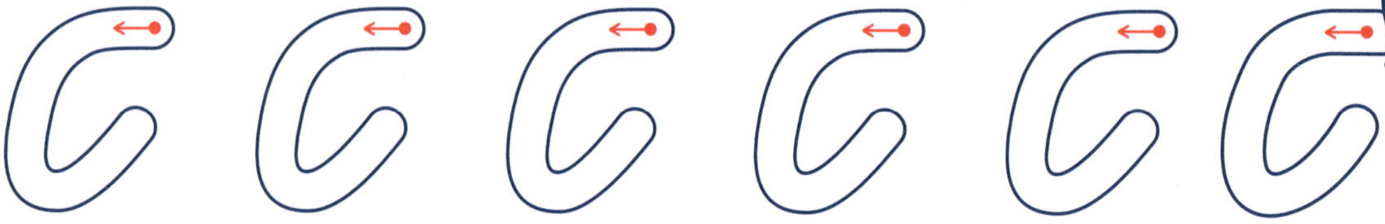

cat

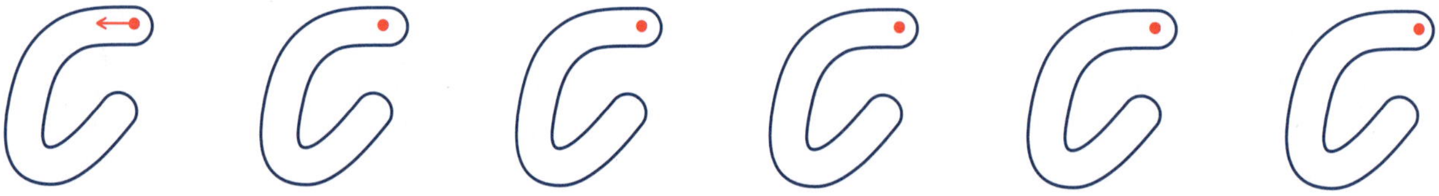

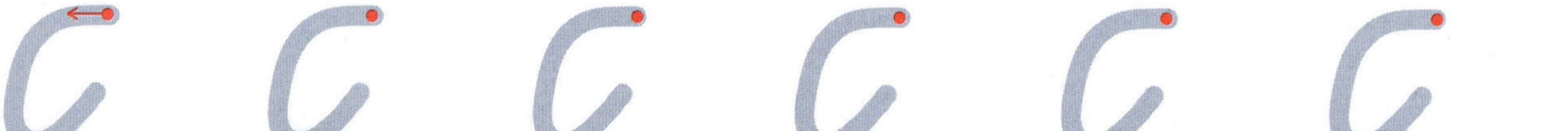

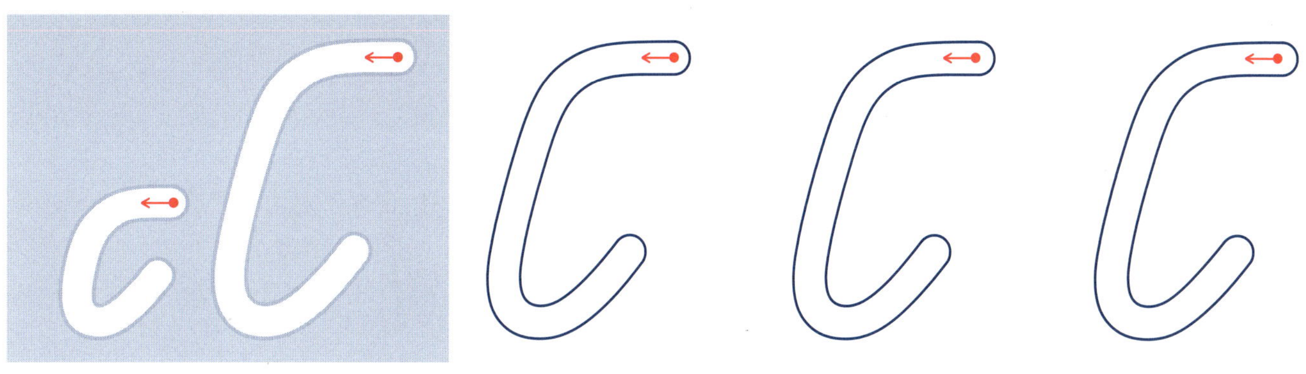

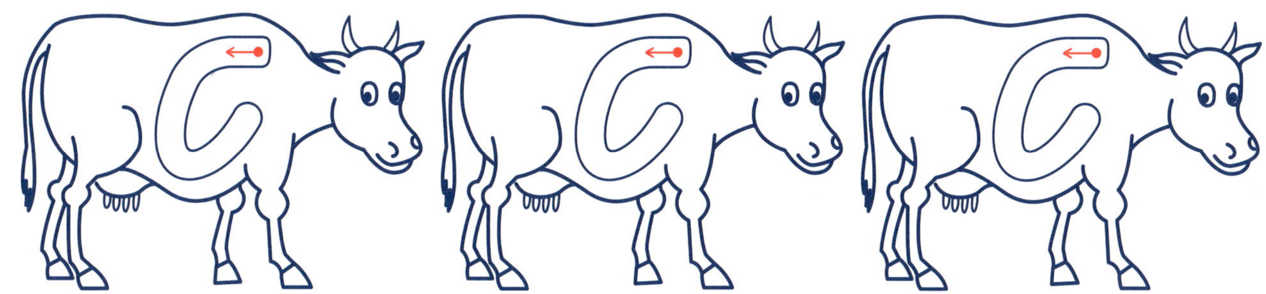

cow

car

Trace the letter.

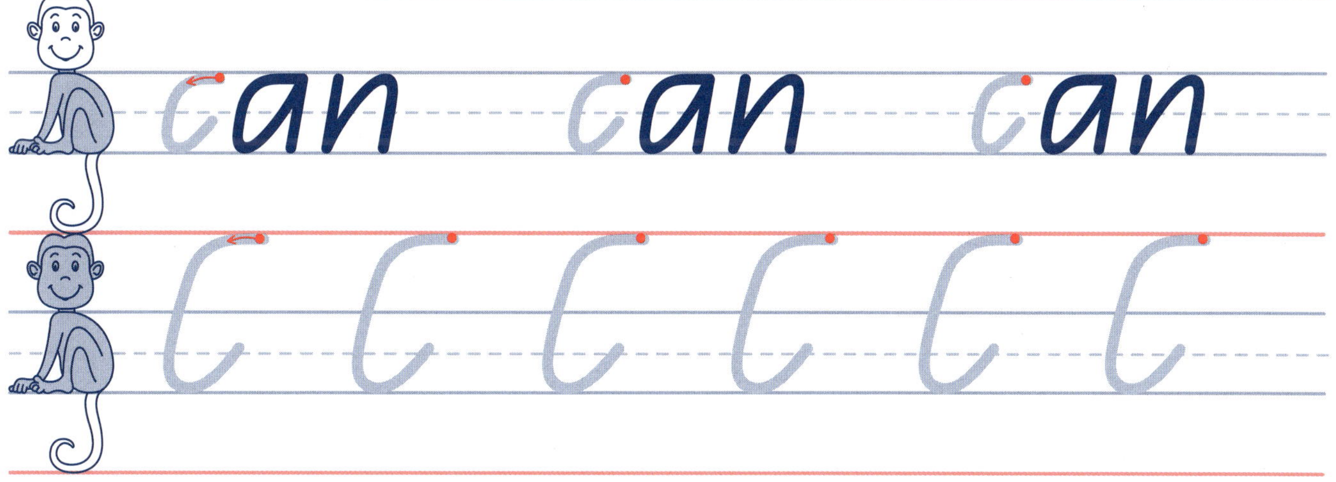

duck

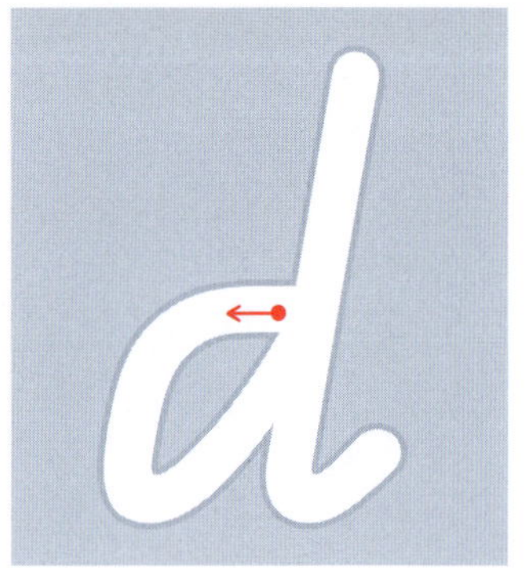

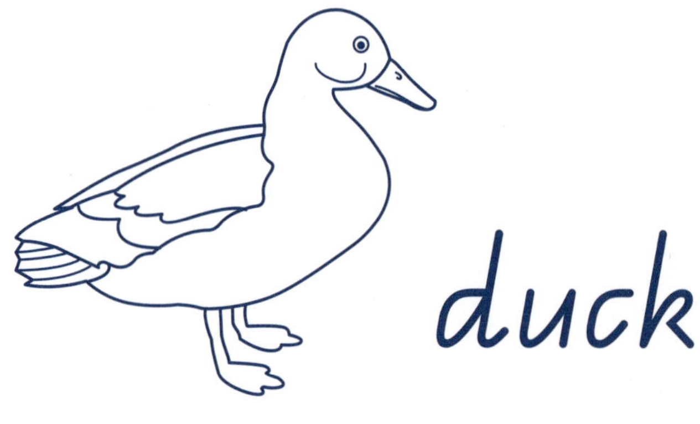

Start at the red dot. Follow the arrow.

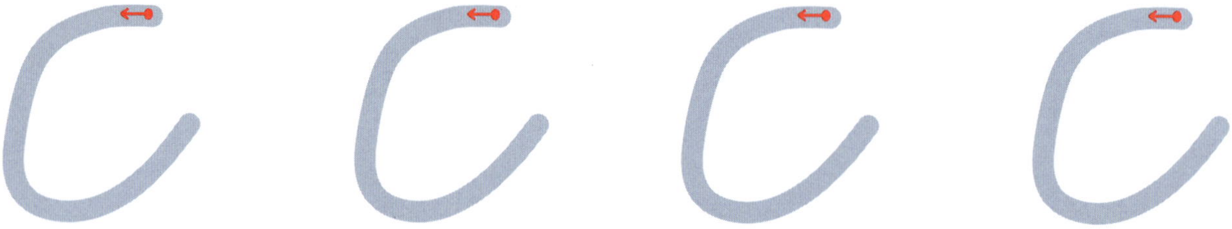

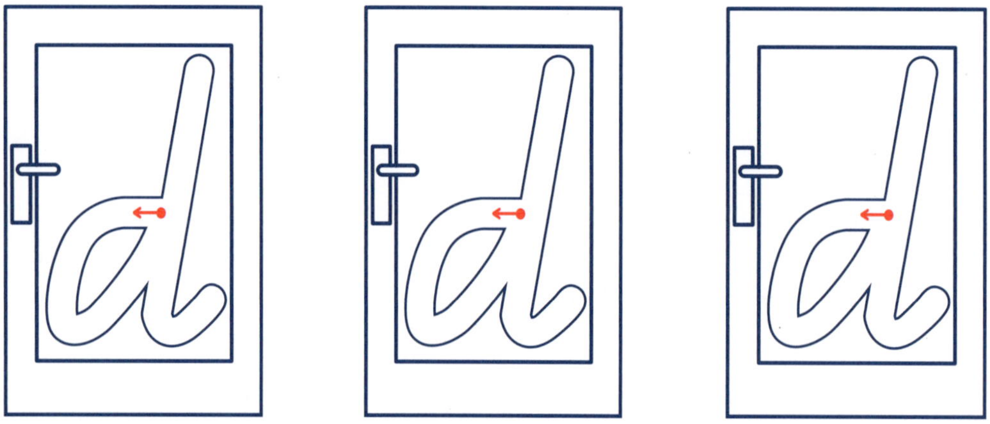

door

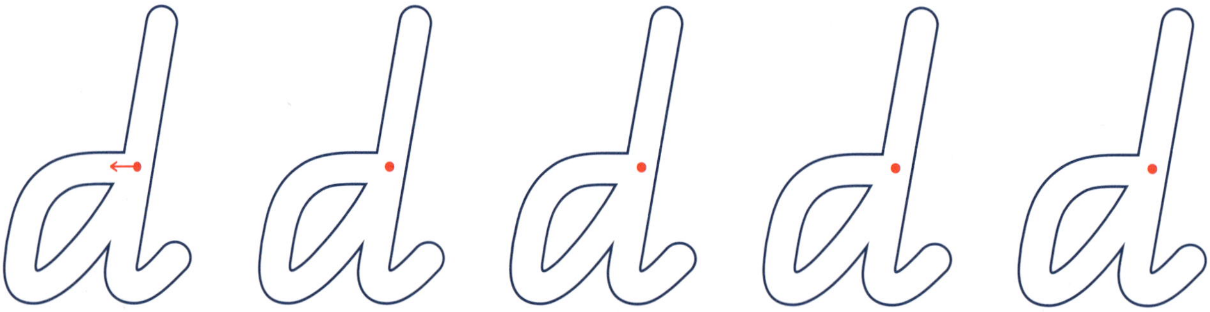

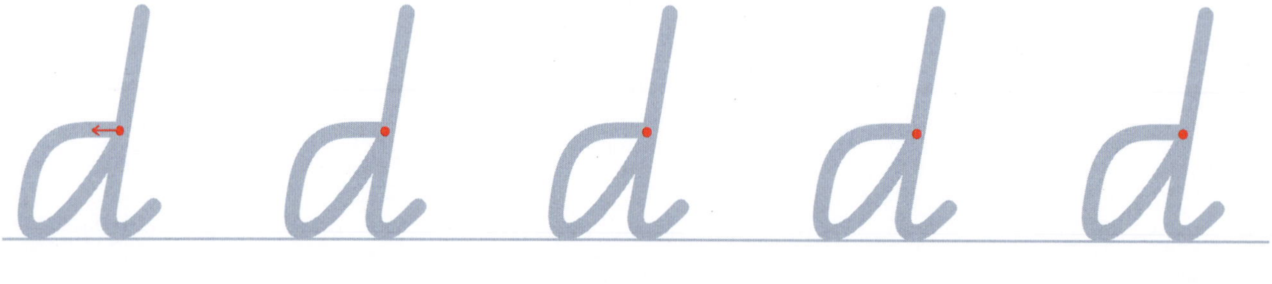

dD DDD

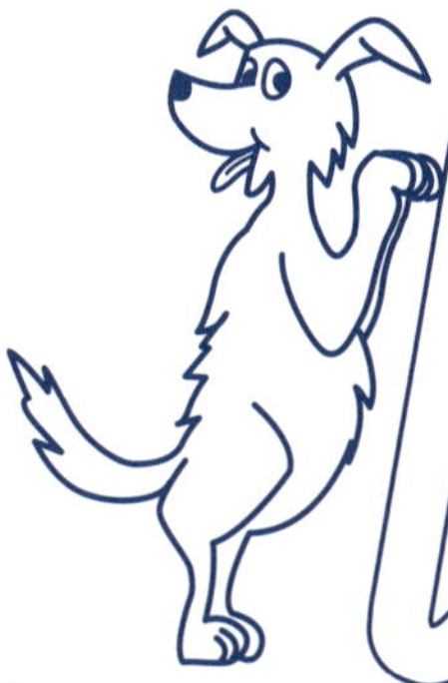

l l l l l l

dog

dinosaur

Trace the letter.

queen

Start at the red dot. Follow the arrow.

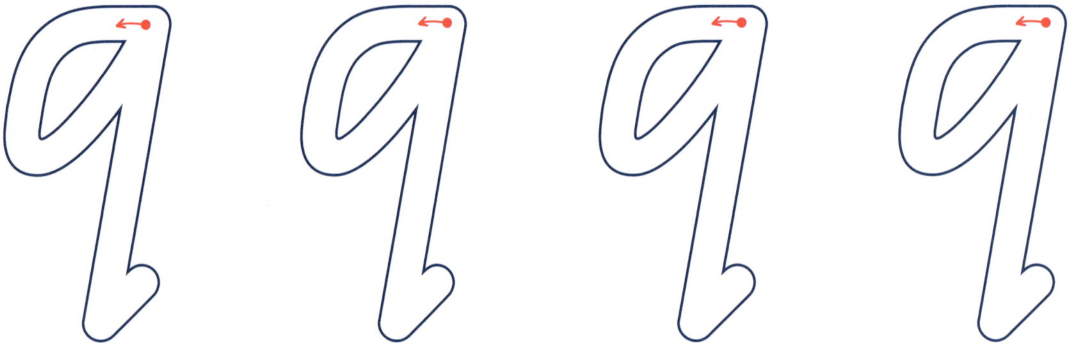

queen

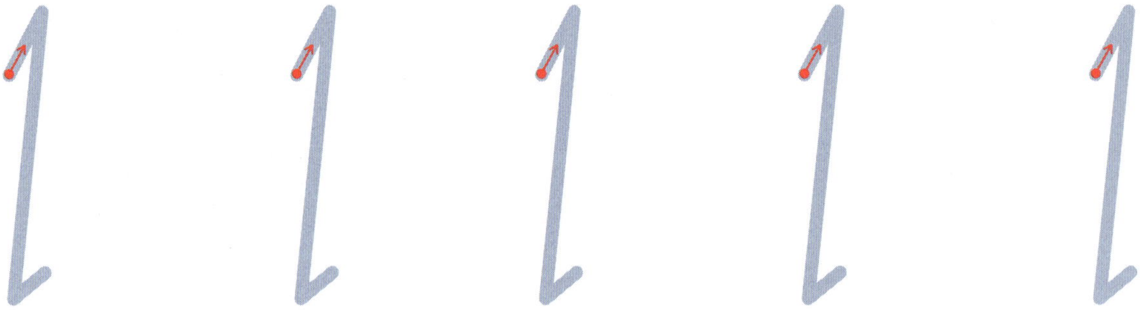

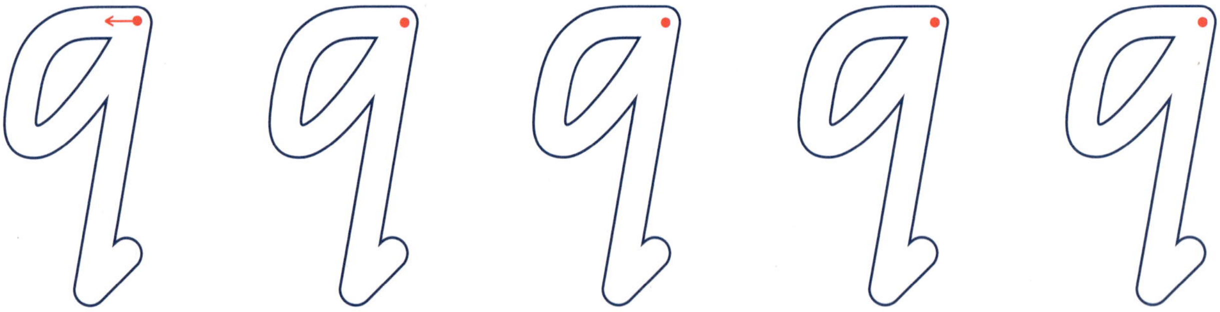

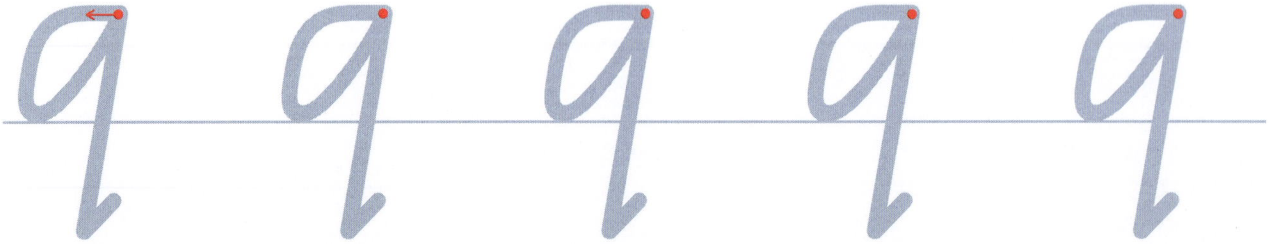

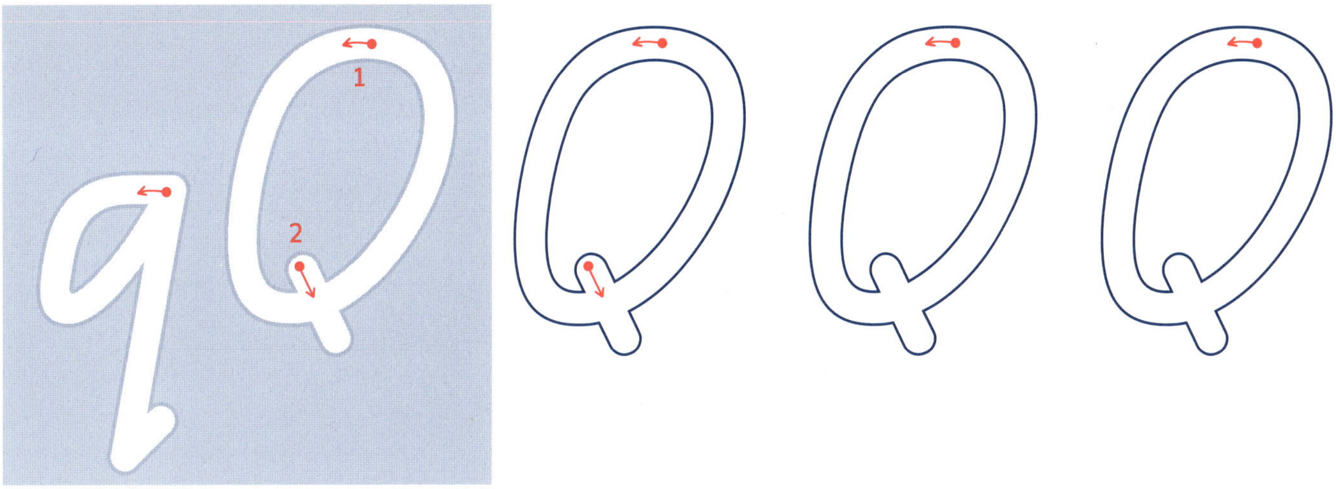

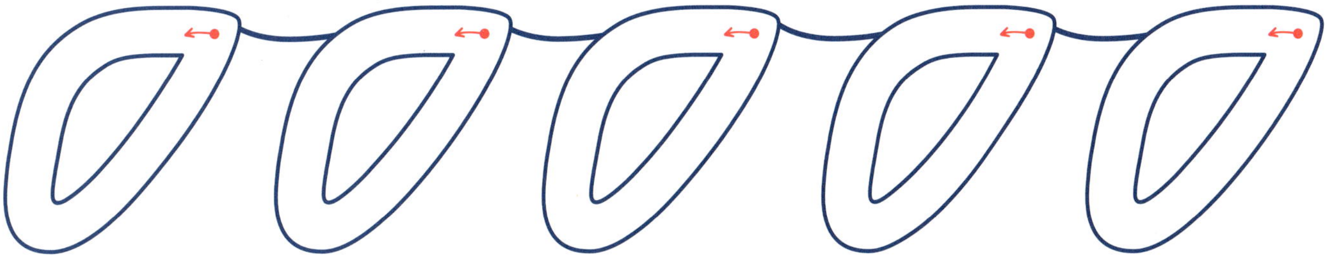

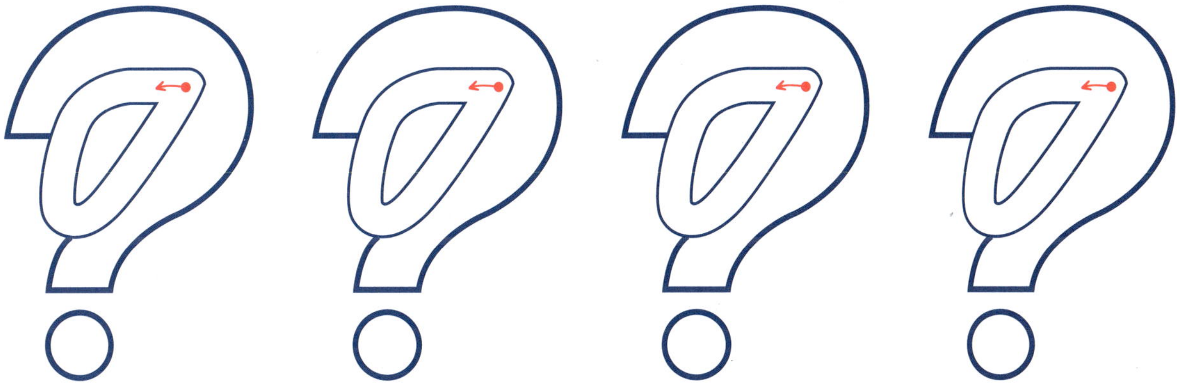

q Q

question mark

Trace the letter.

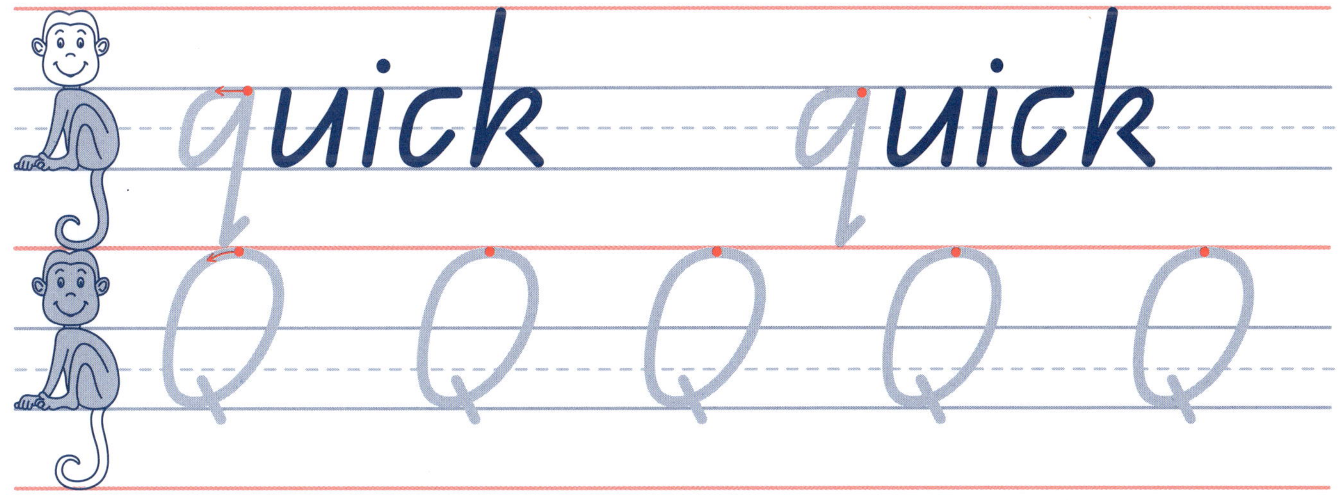

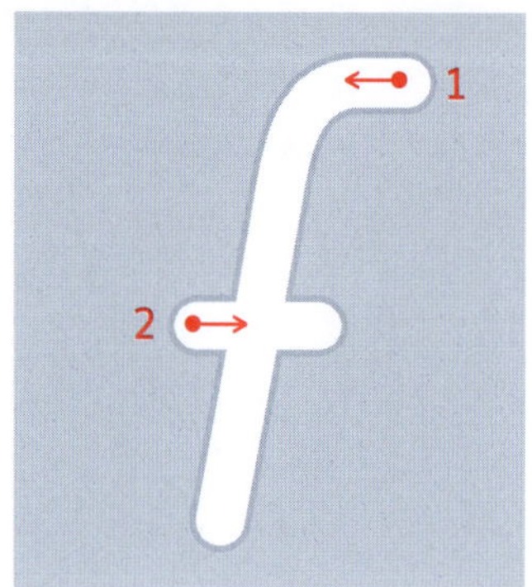

fish

Start at the red dot. Follow the arrow.

feather

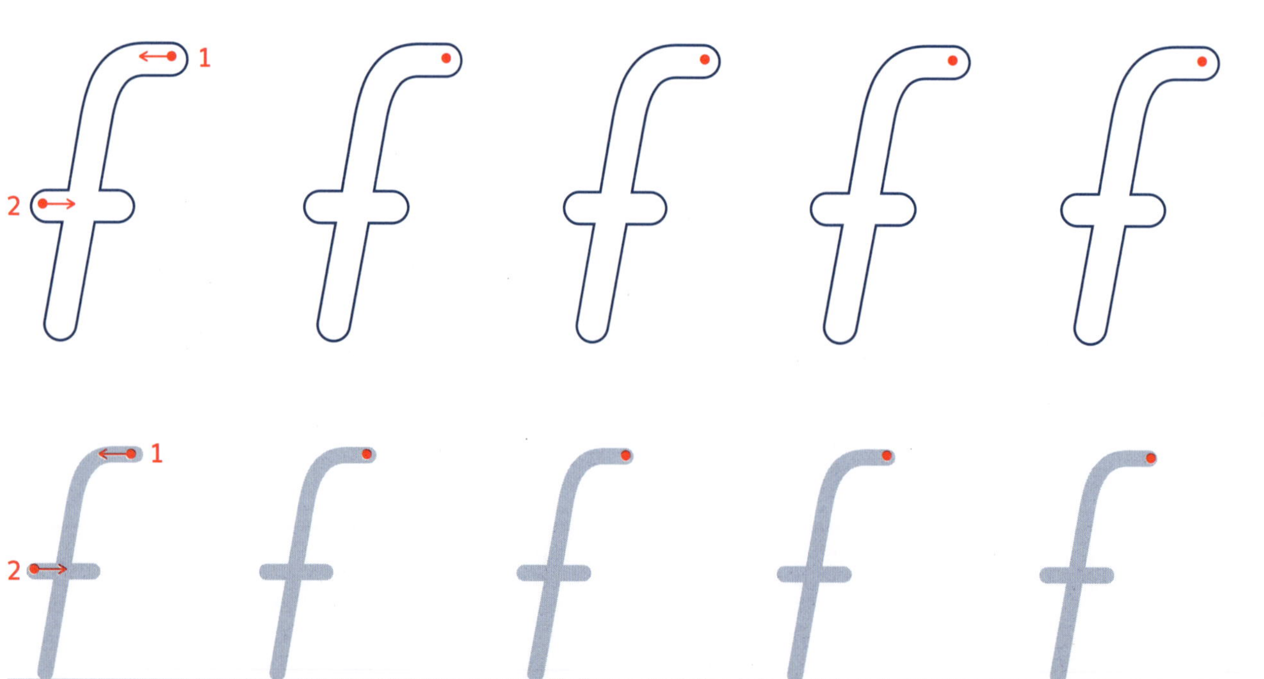

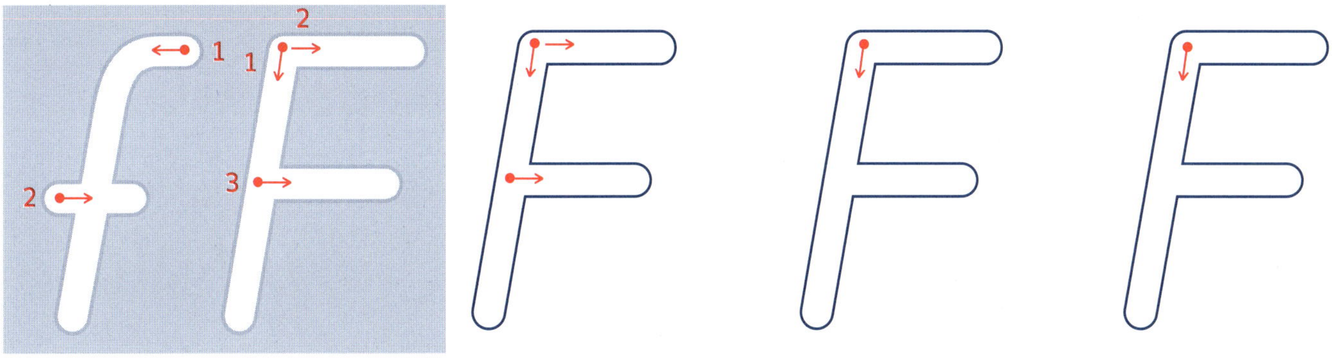

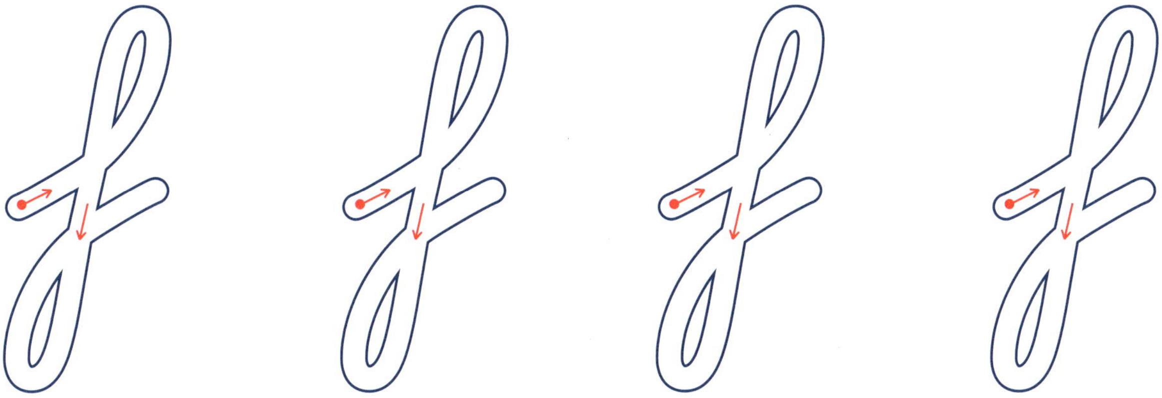

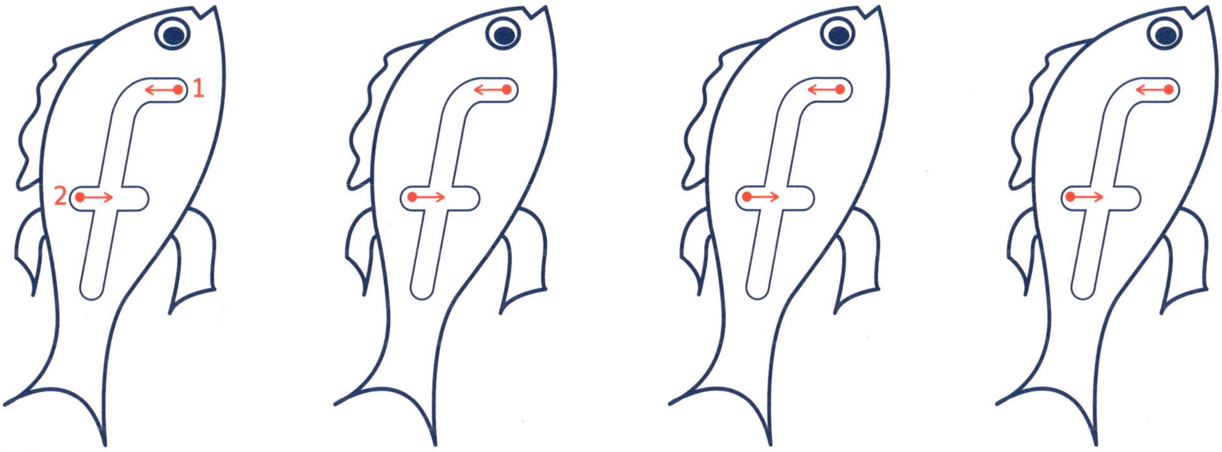

fish

Trace the letter.

o

outside

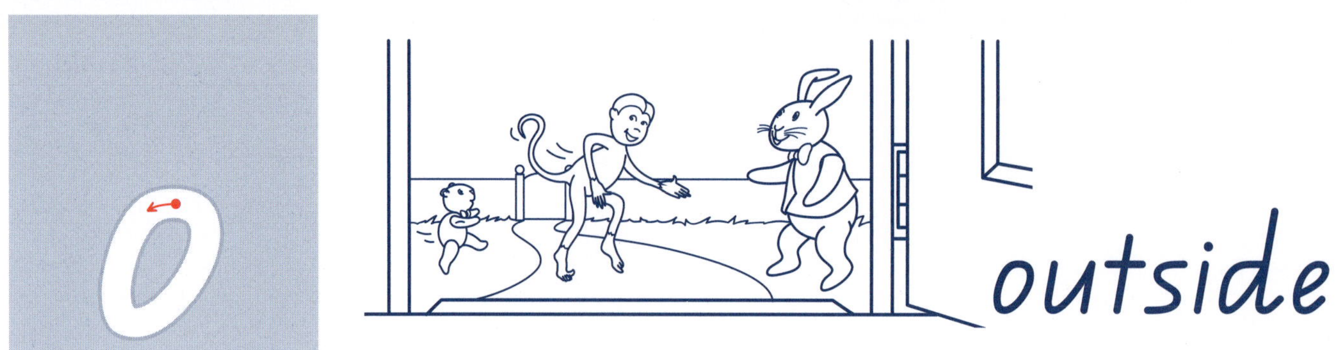

Start at the red dot. Follow the arrow.

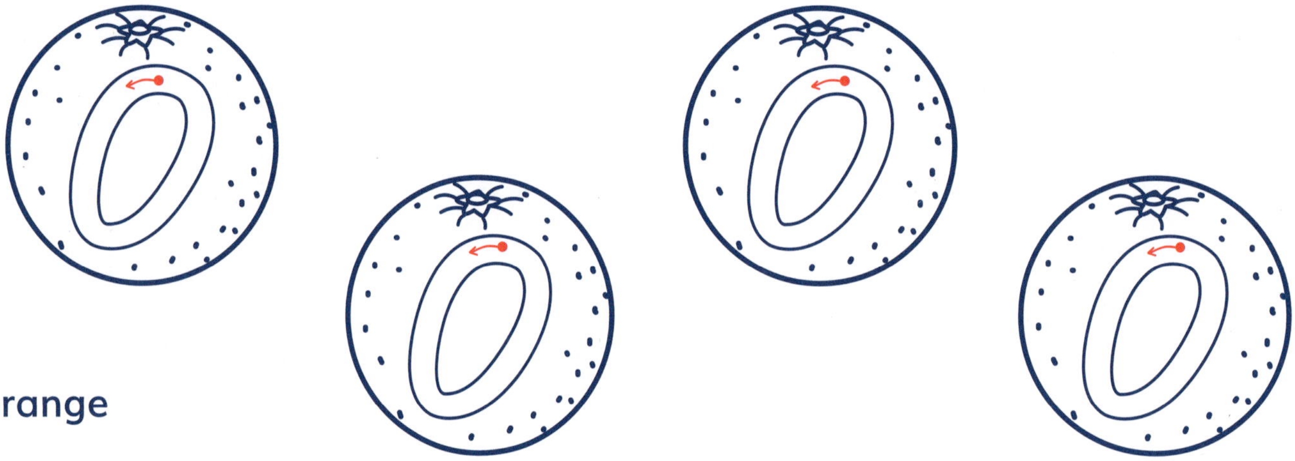

orange

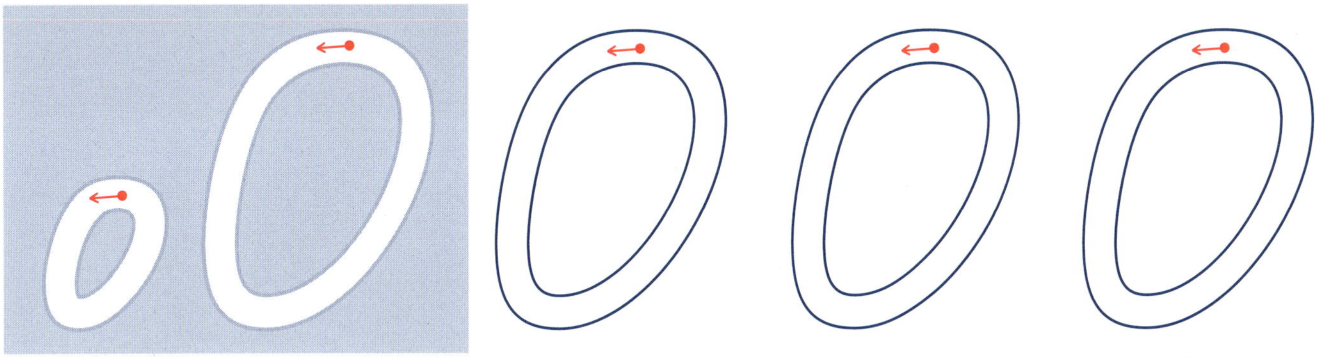

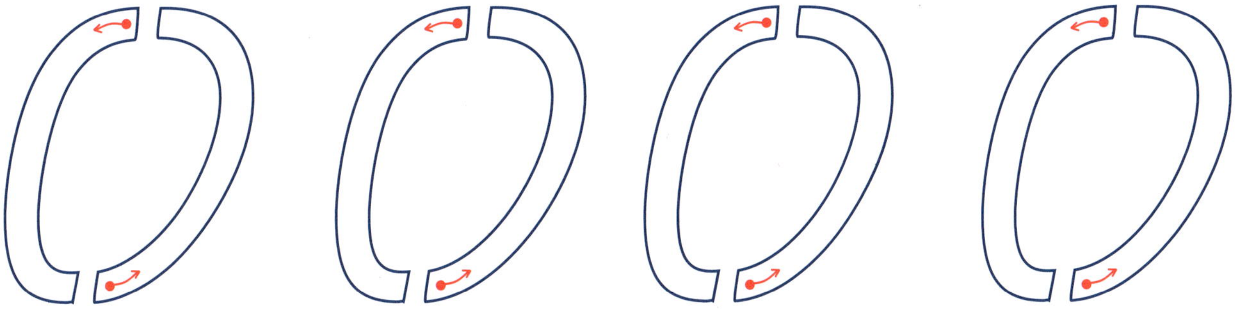

octopus

Trace the letter.

e

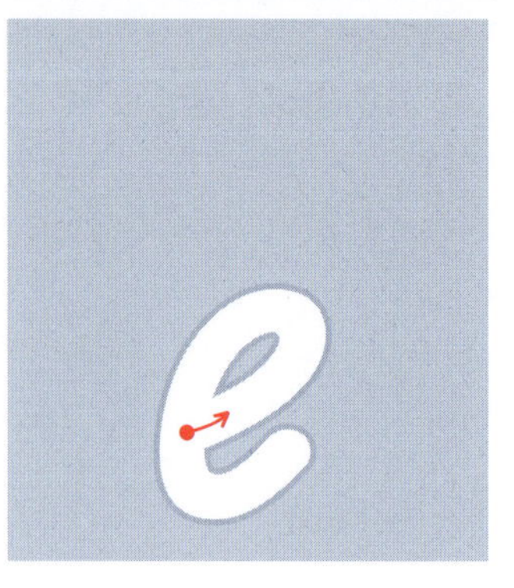

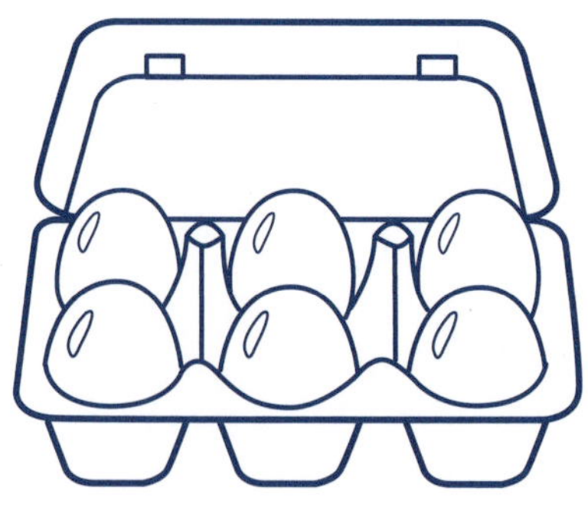

eggs

Start at the red dot. Follow the arrow.

ele ele

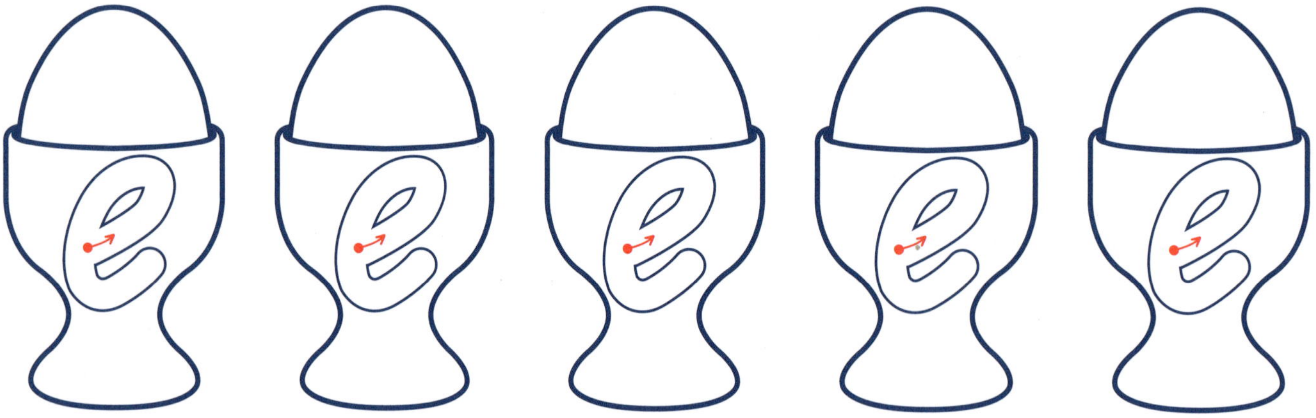

egg

e e e e e

e e e e e

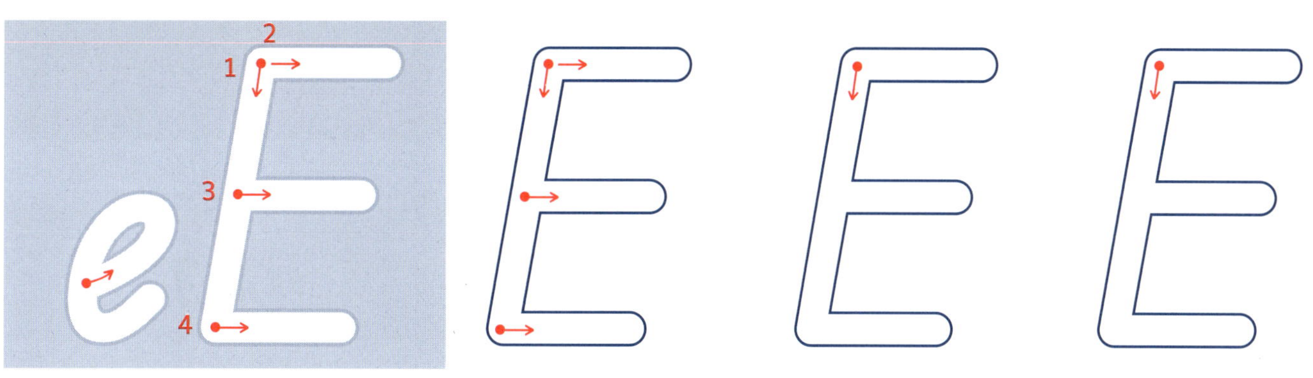

elephant

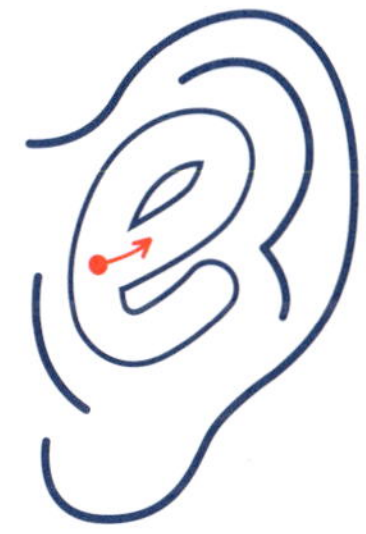
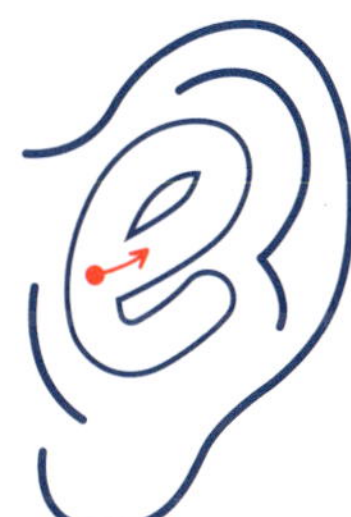
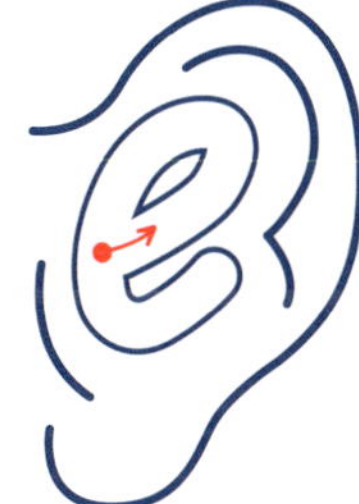
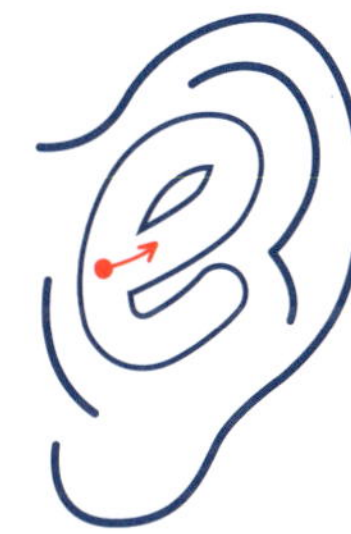
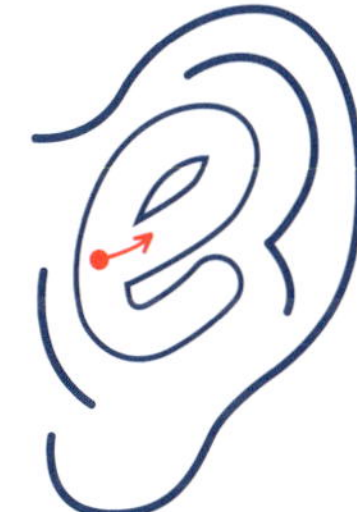

ear

get.ga/PMWA5

Trace the letter.

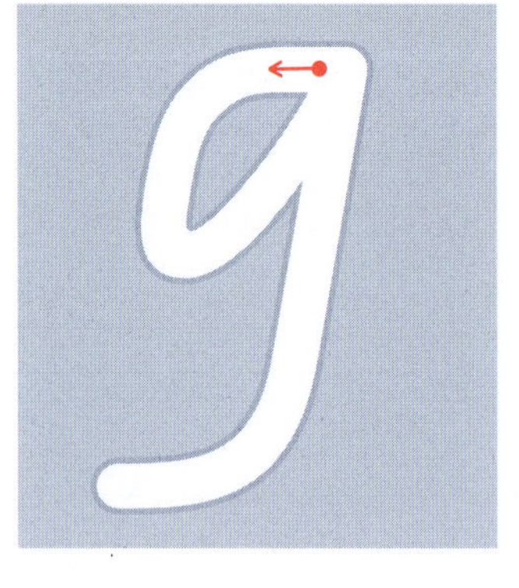

Start at the red dot. Follow the arrow.

garden

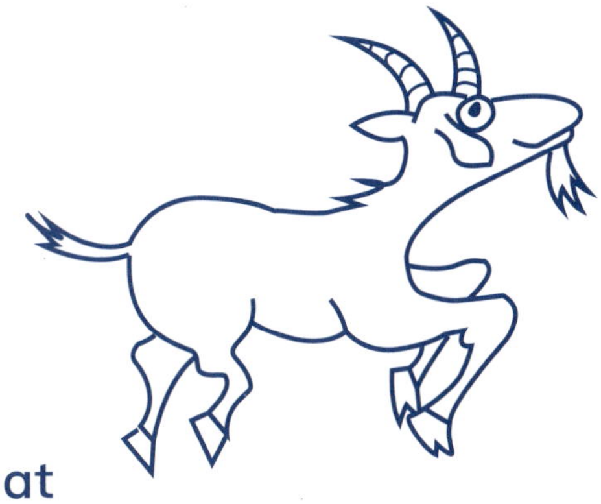

goat

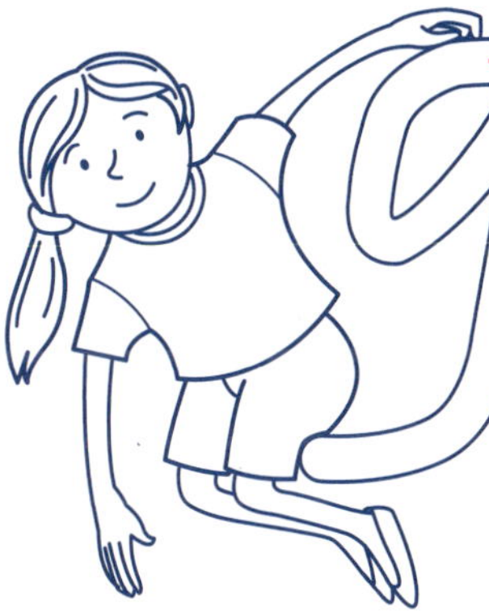

girl

Trace the letter.

get get get get

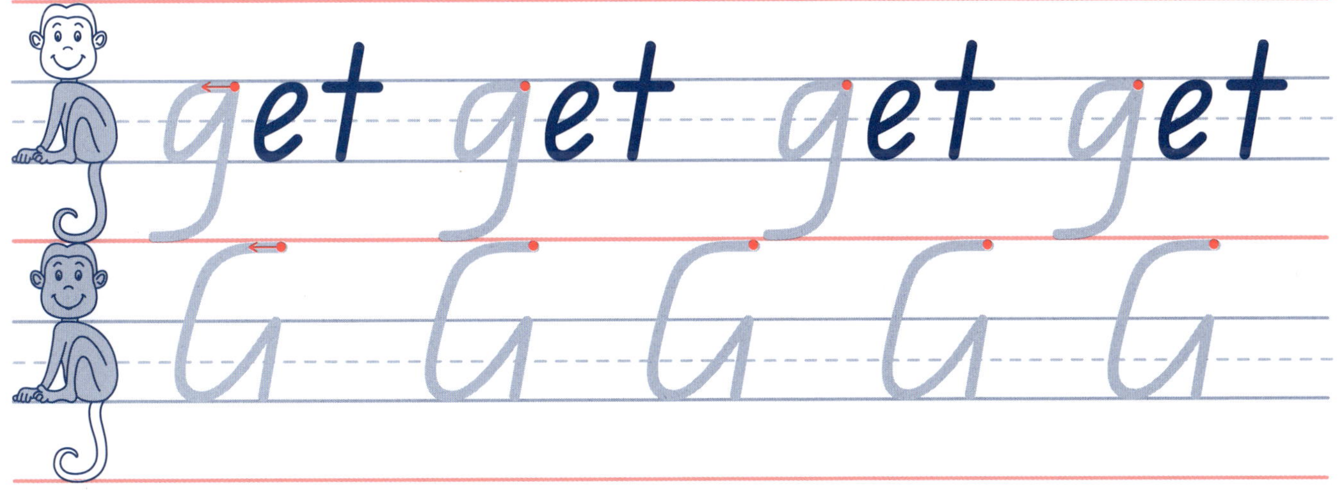

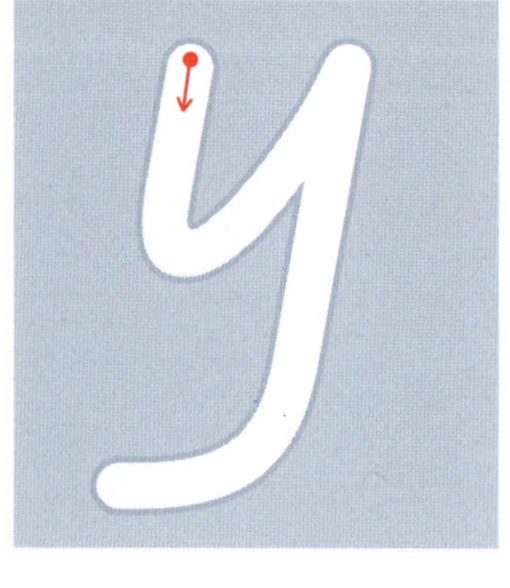

Start at the red dot. Follow the arrow.

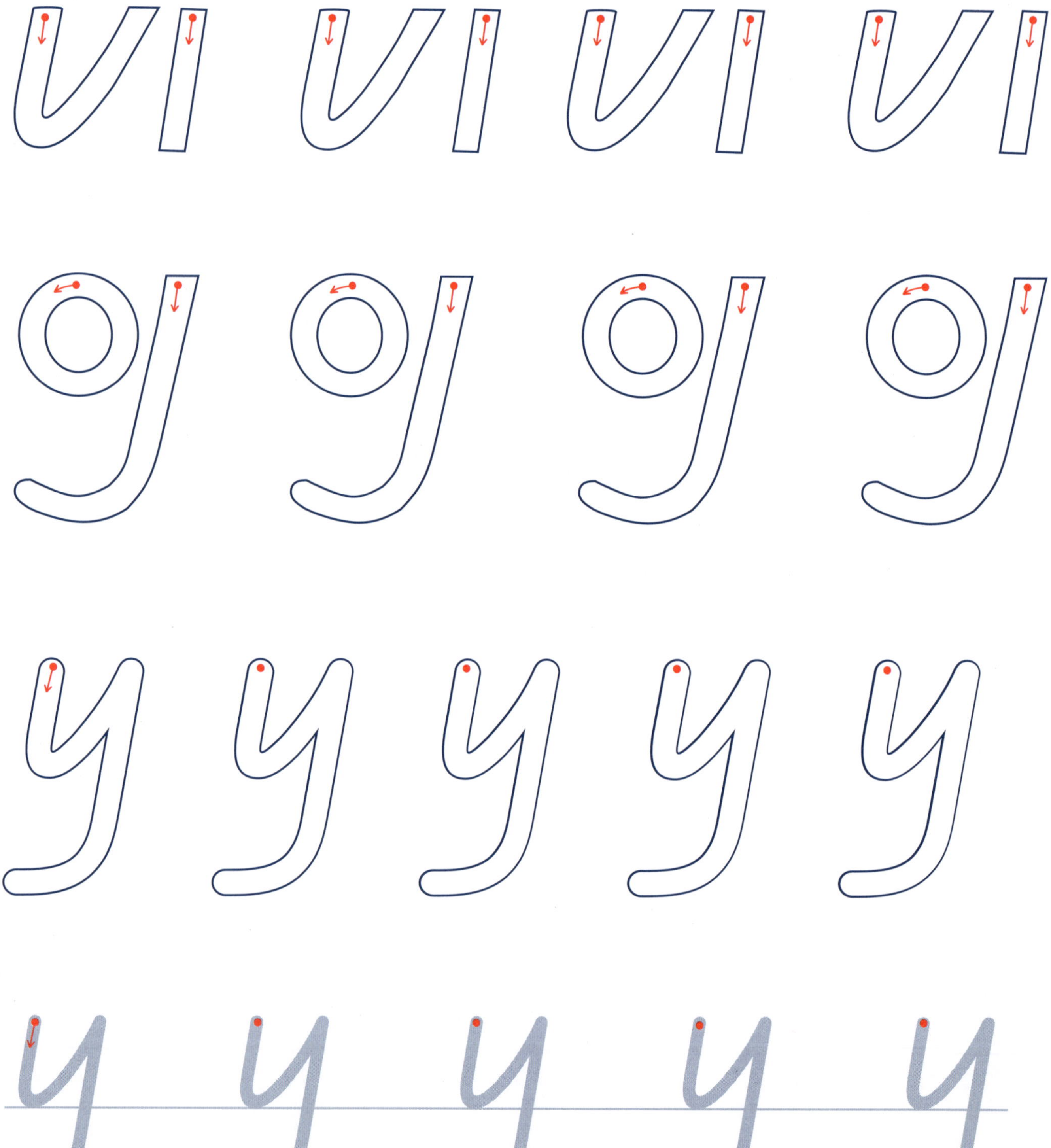

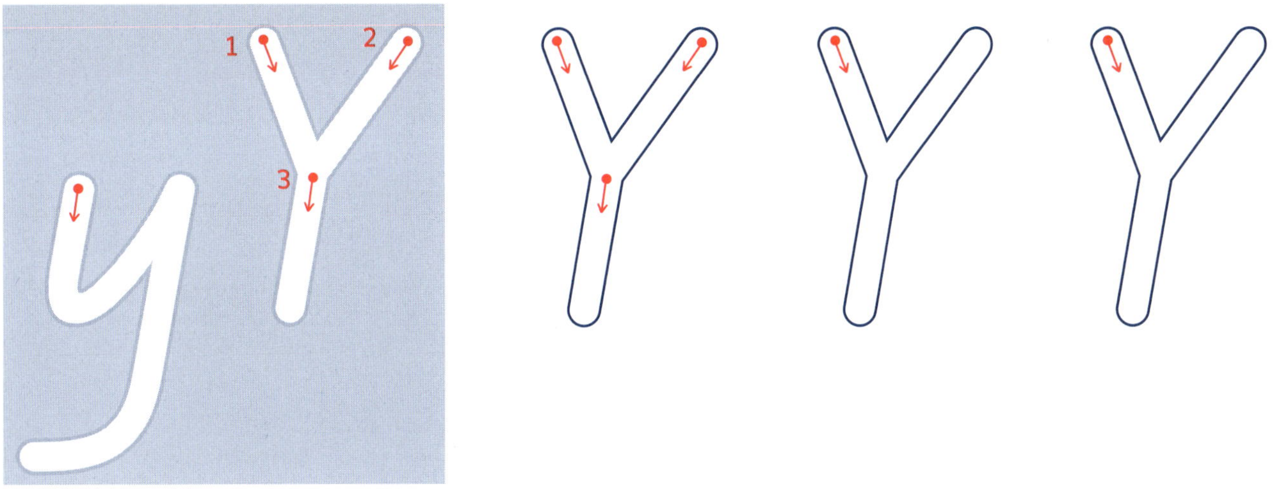

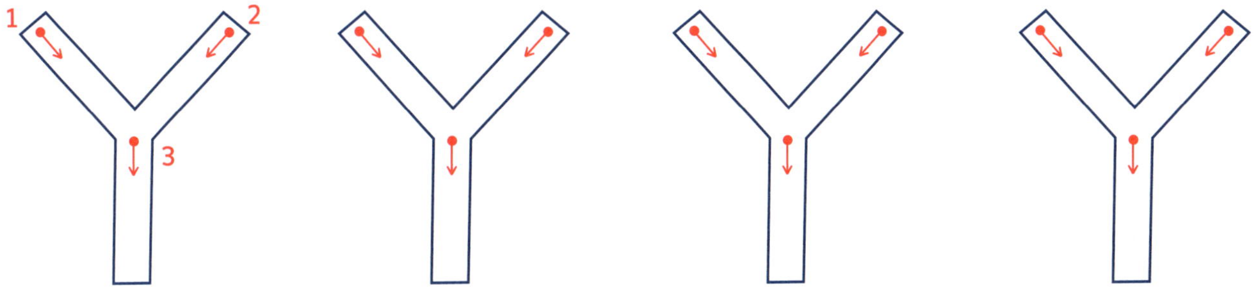

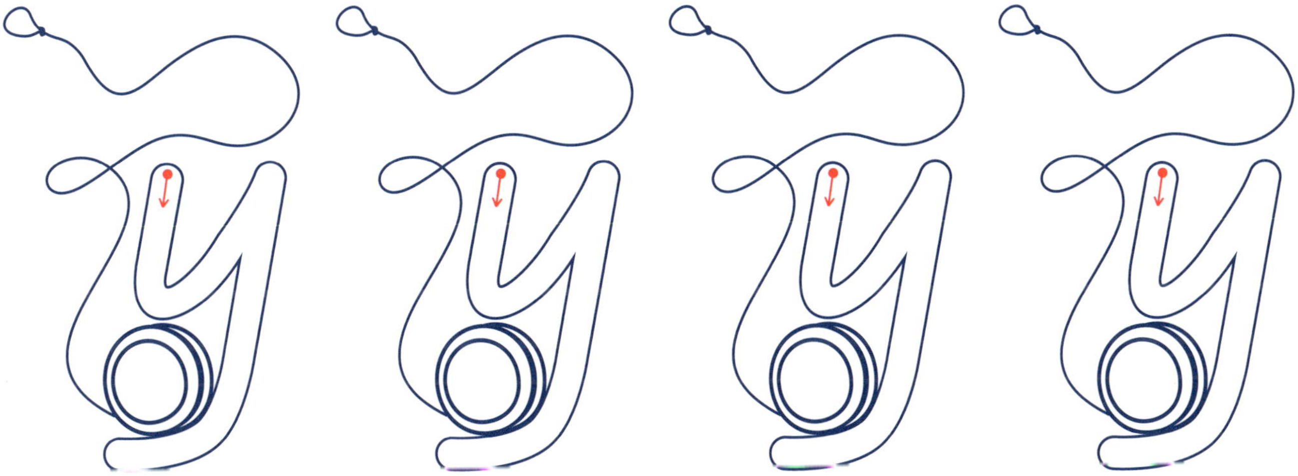

yY

1 2 3

Y Y Y Y

1 2 3

Y Y Y Y

y y y y

yo-yo

Trace the letter.

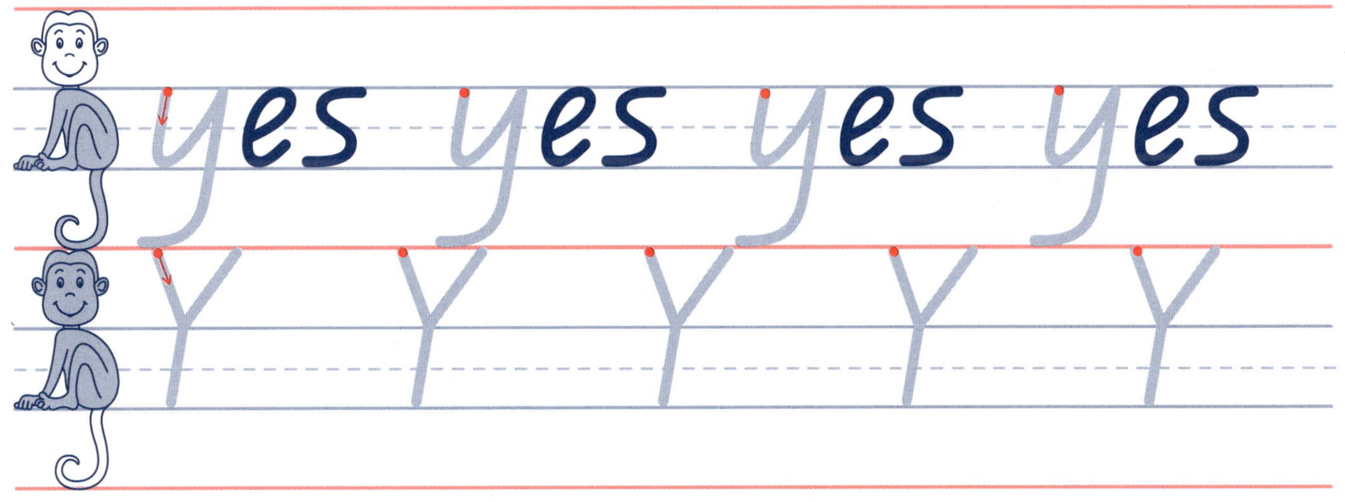

sun

Start at the red dot. Follow the arrow.

snake

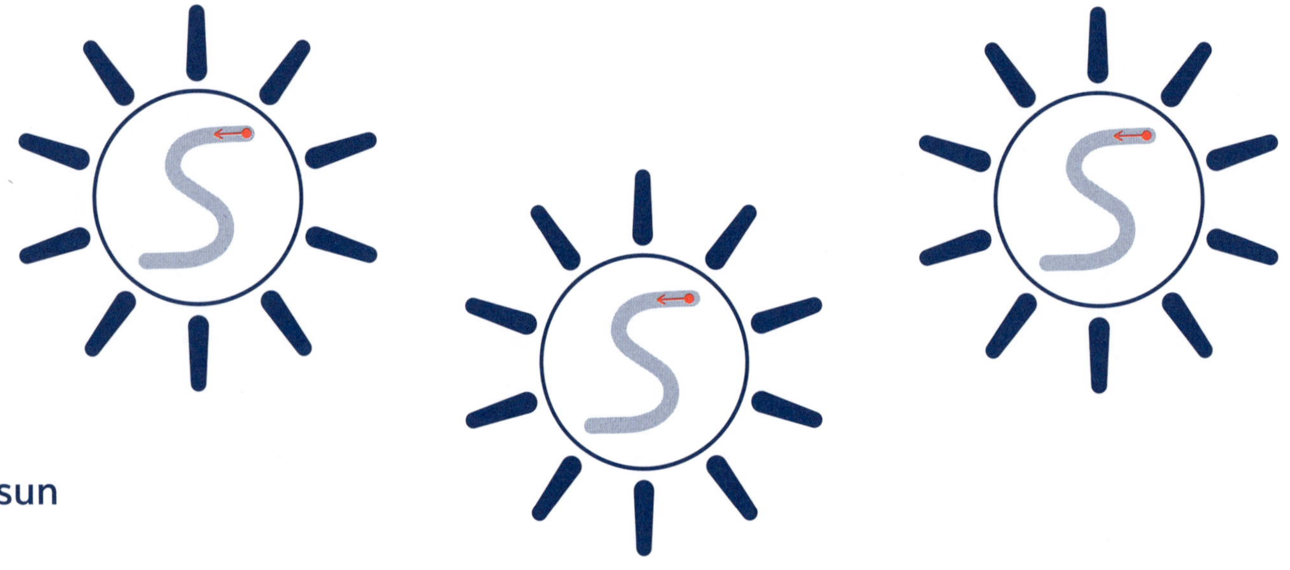

sun

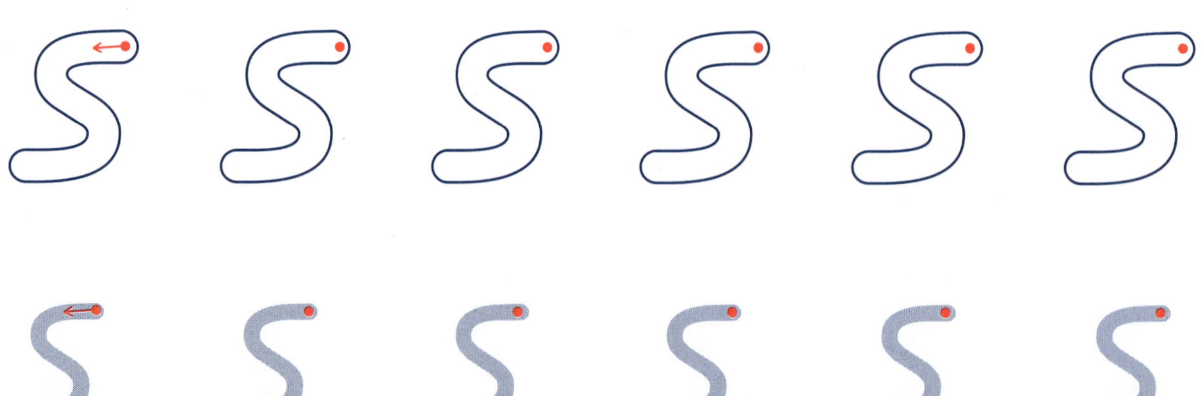

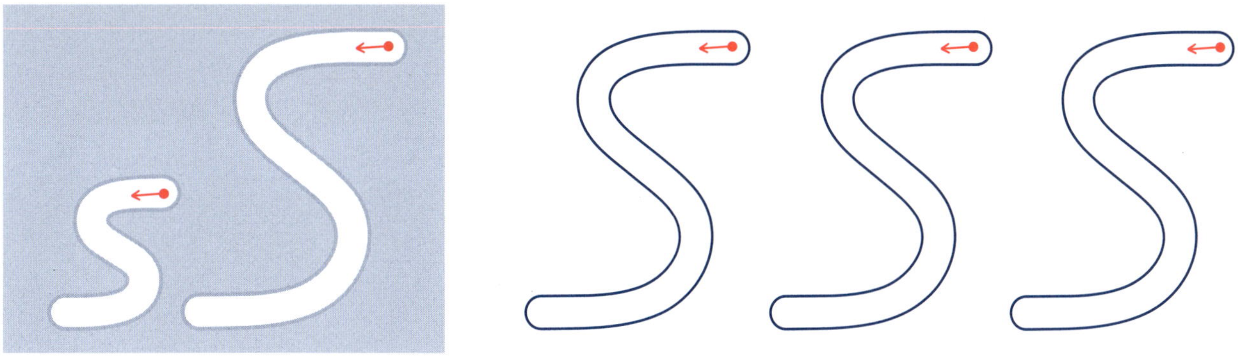

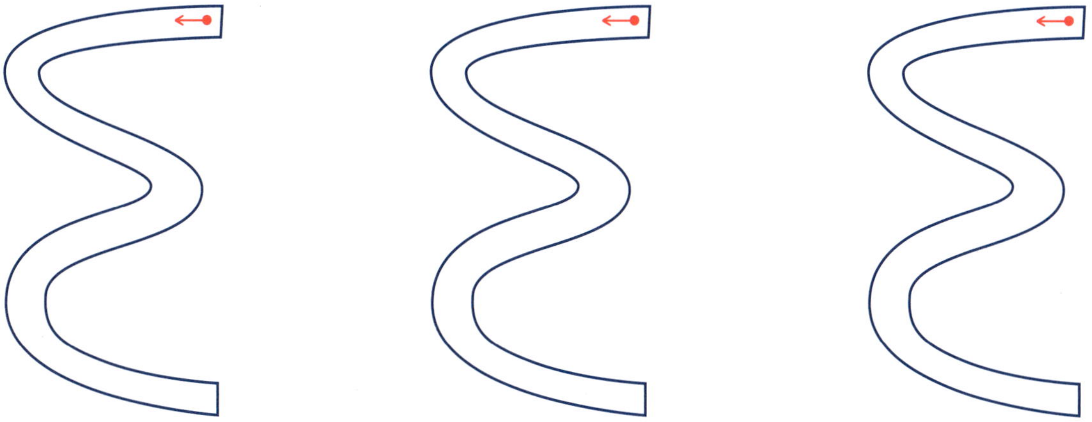

splash

get.ga/PMWA6

Trace the letter.

Trace and copy.

1 one

2 two

3 three

4 four

5 five

Trace and copy.

6 six

7 seven

8 eight

9 nine

10 ten

get.ga/PMWA7

Teacher observation guide

Student is: left-handed ☐ right-handed ☐

Student demonstrates correct posture, paper position and pencil grip. ☐

Student is stroking from top to bottom. ☐

Student is stroking from left to right. ☐

Student is tracking accurately using starting dots and arrows. ☐

Student is tracing accurately using starting dots and arrows. ☐

Student follows simple verbal rehearsals to form letters. ☐

Student forms lower-case letters with accuracy:

a	b	c	d	e	f	g	h	i	j	k	l	m	n	o	p	q	r	s	t	u	v	w	x	y	z

Student forms capital letters with accuracy:

A	B	C	D	E	F	G	H	I	J	K	L	M	N	O	P	Q	R	S	T	U	V	W	X	Y	Z

Student can write the numerals 1–10. ☐

Student uses head, body and tail character to describe the spatial properties of letters. ☐

Student has a growing ability to handwrite within lines. ☐

Notes:

....

....

....

....

Date: ....

CERTIFICATE

get.ga/PMWC1